ABANDONMENT
They abandoned God. Judg. 2:12–13
Though parents forsake you, God will not. Ps. 27:10
"Never will I leave you." Heb. 13:5
Forsaken your first love. Rev. 2:4

ABIDING IN CHRIST
Makes us fruitful. John 15:5
Live in Jesus. 1 John 2:6, 28

ABORTION
Knitted together in womb. Ps. 139:13–16
"Before I formed you in the womb, I knew you." Jer. 1:5
Purposed by God before birth. Gal. 1:15

ABUSE
God sees and helps victims. Ps. 10:14–15
Lord hates lovers of violence. Ps. 11:5
God will avenge. 2 Thess. 1:6

ABUSE, SUBSTANCE
See ADDICTION; DRUNKENNESS.

ACCEPTANCE
Accept wise words. Prov. 4:10
Accept the Word of God. Mark 4:20
Accept those with weak faith. Rom. 14:1
Accept one another. Rom. 15:7

ACCOUNTABILITY
Warn the wicked. Ezek. 33:8
All will give account to God. Rom. 14:12
Confess sins to one another. James 5:16

ADDICTION
Christ made us free. Gal. 5:1
People are slaves to whatever has mastered them. 2 Peter 2:19
See also DRUNKENNESS.

ADOLESCENCE *See* YOUTH.

ADOPTION
"You are my son." Ps. 2:7
We cry, "Abba, Father." Rom. 8:15
Adoption to sonship. Rom. 8:23
Adoption was predestined. Eph. 1:5

ADORATION
God has done great things. Deut. 10:21
Glory is due God's name. 1 Chron. 16:29
Every knee will bow. Phil. 2:10
See also PRAISE; WORSHIP.

ADULTERY
You shall not commit adultery. Ex. 20:14
Adultery in the heart. Matt. 5:28
Will not inherit God's kingdom. 1 Cor. 6:9
Honor marriage. Heb. 13:4

ADVENT *See* CHRISTMAS.

ADVICE
Fools despise advice. Prov. 1:7
Victory through advisers. Prov. 11:14
Listen to advice. Prov. 19:20
Be quick to listen. James 1:19
See also GUIDANCE.

ADVOCATE
Rescue the oppressed. Jer. 22:3
Holy Spirit, the Advocate. John 14:26
Jesus is our advocate. 1 John 2:1

ALCOHOL
It is a mocker. Prov. 20:1
Take a little for your stomach. 1 Tim. 5:23
See also Drunkenness; Wine.

ANGELS
Angels sent before you. Ex. 33:2
God will command them. Ps. 91:11
Children's angels in heaven. Matt. 18:10
Angels worship Jesus. Heb. 1:6
Ministering spirits. Heb. 1:14
Entertain angels unawares. Heb. 13:2
Michael the Archangel. Jude 1:9

ANGER
A fool gives full vent to it. Prov 29:11
Don't rush to be angry. Eccl. 7:9
Who can abide God's anger? Nah. 1:6
Don't go to bed angry. Eph. 4:26
Get rid of anger. Eph. 4:31
Be slow to become angry. James 1:19–20

ANIMALS
God created every creature. Gen. 1:20–25
Adam named the animals. Gen. 2:20
Two of every kind in Noah's ark. Gen. 7:15
See also Birds; Fish.

ANOINTING
Sacred anointing oil. Ex. 29:36; 30:25
Anoint head with oil. Ps. 23:5
Jesus' feet anointed. John 12:3
Anointing with the oil of joy. Heb. 1:9
Anoint the sick with oil. James 5:14

ANTICHRIST
The abomination of desolation. Dan. 12:11; Matt. 24:15
Antichrist will come. 1 John 2:18
Many antichrists have come. 1 John 2:18
The spirit of antichrist is here. 1 John 4:3
Deceivers are antichrists. 2 John 1:7

ANXIETY
Heaviness in the heart. Prov. 12:25
Rest for anxious souls. Matt. 11:28–30
Daily pressures. 2 Cor. 11:28
Don't be anxious about anything, but present requests to God. Phil. 4:6–7
God is on your side. Heb. 13:6
Cast all your anxieties on God. 1 Peter 5:7
See also Stress; Worry.

APOSTASY
Apostasy will reprove you. Jer. 2:19
God will heal apostasy. Hos. 14:4
Some will give up the faith. 1 Tim. 4:1
See also Backsliding.

APOSTLES
Twelve disciples/apostles. Matt. 10:2–4
Mathias chosen by lot. Acts 1:26
Paul, apostle to Gentiles. Rom. 11:13
Gift of apostleship 1 Cor. 12:28; Eph. 4:11
False apostles. 2 Cor. 11:13

ARK OF THE COVENANT
Instructions for the ark. Ex. 25:10–22
The ark set in the temple. 1 Kings 6:19
See also Mercy Seat.

ARMAGEDDON
A great battle will be fought. Rev. 16:16
See also End Times.

ARMOR OF GOD

Armor of light. Rom. 13:12
Armor of righteousness. 2 Cor. 6:7
Put on the whole armor. Eph. 6:11–17
See also SPIRITUAL WARFARE.

ARROGANCE

Don't speak proudly. 1 Sam. 2:3
Be wise to hate it. Prov. 8:13
God will end it. Isa. 13:11
Arrogant schemes. James 4:16
See also BOASTING; PRIDE.

ASCENSION OF CHRIST

To heaven. Luke 24:50–51; Acts 1:9

ASSURANCE OF SALVATION

Not taken from God's hand. John 10:28
There is no condemnation. Rom. 8:1
Nothing can separate us. Rom. 8:38–39
God will carry it to completion. Phil. 1:6
You have eternal life. 1 John 5:13
See also SALVATION.

ATHEISM

Fool says, "there is no God." Ps. 14:1; 53:1
Understanding is darkened. Eph. 4:18

ATONEMENT

Make atonement for sin. Lev. 4:26
Atonement for all Israel. 2 Chron. 29:24
Received through Jesus. Rom. 5:11

AUTHORITY

All authority is given to Jesus. Matt. 28:18
Authority over the enemy. Luke 10:19
Submit to civil authorities. Rom. 13:1
Pray for those in authority. 1 Tim. 2:1–2
See also DOMINION; GOVERNMENT.

BACKSLIDING

Filled with our own ways. Prov. 14:14
The people refuse to return. Jer. 8:5
God will heal waywardness. Hos. 14:4
"You have left your first love." Rev. 2:4
Lukewarm faith. Rev. 3:15–16
See also APOSTASY.

BACKSTABBING *See* BETRAYAL.

BAPTISM

With Holy Spirit and fire. Matt. 3:11
Jesus was baptized. Matt. 3:16–17; Mark 1:9-11; Luke 3:21–22; John 1:29–34
Baptize disciples. Matt. 28:19–20
Repent and be baptized. Acts 2:38
Buried and raised with Christ. Rom. 6:3–6; Col. 2:12

BEATITUDES

Blessed are the . . . Matt. 5:3–12

BEAUTY

Do not lust after beauty. Prov. 6:25
Beauty is fleeting. Prov. 31:30
Everything beautiful in its time. Eccl. 3:11
Beautiful on the outside, but unclean within. Matt. 23:27
Unfading beauty of gentleness. 1 Peter 3:4

BELIEF *See* Faith.

BELIEVERS *See* Christians.

BETRAYAL
A false witness. Prov. 19:5
Keep confidences. Prov. 25:9
Pray for persecutors. Matt. 5:44
Jesus was betrayed by Judas. Matt. 26:49

BIBLE *See* Scripture.

BIRDS
Valued much more than birds. Matt. 6:26
Be harmless as doves. Matt. 10:16
Soar like eagles. Isa. 40:31

BITTERNESS
Bitter soul is way to death. Job 21:25
Typical of the unrighteous. Rom. 3:11–14
Get rid of bitterness. Eph. 4:31
A root of bitterness. Heb. 12:15
See also Grudges.

BLASPHEMY
Against the Holy Spirit. Matt. 12:31
Jesus wrongly accused. Mark 14:62–64
Characteristic of the beast. Rev. 13:1

BLESSING
"I will bless those who bless you." Gen. 12:1–3; Gal. 3:8
Lord bless you, keep you. Num. 6:24–26
Blessed are the . . . Matt. 5:1–11
Spiritual blessings. Eph. 1:3
Blessings of the gospel. 1 Cor. 9:23
See also Gifts.

BLINDNESS, SPIRITUAL
The blind leading the blind. Matt. 15:14
Blind minds of unbelievers. 2 Cor. 4:4
See also Eyes; Sight.

BLOOD
Life is in the blood. Lev. 17:11
Jesus' blood of the covenant. Matt. 26:28
In prayer, Jesus' sweat was like drops of blood. Luke 22:44
Redemption through Jesus' blood. Eph. 1:7
No forgiveness without the shedding of blood. Heb. 9:22
Redeemed by Christ's. 1 Peter 1:18–19
Washed in blood of the Lamb. Rev. 7:14

BOASTING
Stop boasting. Ps. 75:4
Don't boast about future. Prov. 27:1
Boast not in wisdom, strength, or riches. Jer. 9:23
Boasting is not good. 1 Cor. 5:6
See also Arrogance; Pride.

BODY
"This is my body, given for you." Matt. 26:26; Mark 14:22; Luke 22:19; 1 Cor. 11:24
Bodies as living sacrifices. Rom. 12:1
Honor God with your body. 1 Cor. 6:18–20
See also Church.

BOOK OF LIFE
Blotted out of the book. Ps. 69:28
Believers in the book. Phil. 4:3
Names never blotted out. Rev. 3:5
Lamb's book of life. Rev. 13:8; 21:27

BORN AGAIN
You must be born again. John 3:1–8
New birth into a living hope. 1 Peter 1:3
Through the word of God. 1 Peter 1:23

Believers are born of God. 1 John 5:1
See also SALVATION.

BOUNDARIES

God set the earth's boundaries. Ps. 74:17
Guard your heart. Prov. 4:23
Let your yes be yes; no be no. Matt. 5:37

BREAD

We do not live on bread alone. Deut. 8:3; Luke 4:4
Daily bread. Prov. 30:8; Matt. 6:11
Bread of God from heaven. John 6:33
"I am the bread of life." John 6:48
Symbolic of Jesus' body. 1 Cor. 11:24

BRIBERY

Hate dishonest gain. Ex. 18:21
God takes no bribes. Deut. 10:17
The wicked accept bribes. Prov. 17:23
Bribes destroy a country. Prov. 29:4
God's gifts are free. Acts 8:18–25

BROTHERS AND SISTERS

See FAMILY.

BULLYING *See* ABUSE; SPEECH.

BUSINESS

Work with willing hands. Prov. 31:13
"I must be about my father's business." Luke 2:49
Do all in the name of the Lord. Col. 3:17
Treat workers fairly. Col. 4:1

BUSYNESS

Martha was distracted. Luke 10:40
Jesus retreated to a solitary place. Mark 6:31–32

CALLING

God called the boy Samuel. 1 Sam. 3:10
Jesus called his disciples. Matt. 4:18–22
Live worthy of your calling. Eph. 4:1
The high calling of God. Phil. 3:14
Confirm your calling. 2 Peter 1:10
See also MINISTRY.

CAPITAL PUNISHMENT

Whoever sheds human blood. Gen. 9:6
Murderers put to death. Lev. 24:17
Turn the other cheek. Matt. 5:38–41
See also MURDER.

CELEBRATION

David danced in celebration. 2 Sam. 6:16
Celebration for son's return. Luke 15:23
Do all for God's glory. 1 Cor. 10:31

CELIBACY

For the sake of God's kingdom. Matt. 19:12
The gift of celibacy. 1 Cor. 7:5–7

CHARACTER

God sees the heart. 1 Sam. 16:7
A wife of good character. Prov. 12:4
Endurance produces character. Rom. 5:4
See also REPUTATION.

CHARITY *See* GIVING; LOVE.

CHEATING
A cheat is cursed. Mal. 1:14
Cheating other Christians. 1 Cor. 6:8
See also DECEPTION; STEALING.

CHEERFUL
Have a merry heart. Prov. 15:13
Cheerfully show mercy. Rom. 12:8
God loves a cheerful giver. 2 Cor. 9:7
See also HAPPINESS; JOY.

CHILDBIRTH
Pain in childbirth. Gen. 3:16
Saved through childbirth. 1 Tim. 2:15

CHILDREN
Are a heritage from God. Ps. 127:3
Jesus' warning to those who cause children to stumble. Matt. 18:6; Mark 9:42
"Let the little children come to me." Matt. 19:14
God's kingdom is theirs. Luke 18:16
Children, obey your parents. Eph. 6:1

CHILDREN OF GOD
Peacemakers are. Matt. 5:9
The right to become. John 1:12
Spirit confirms that we are. Rom. 8:16
Called children through faith. Gal. 3:26

CHRIST *See* JESUS; MESSIAH.

CHRISTIANS
Unity among Christians. Acts 2:44; 4:32
New believers in Christ. Acts 8:15
Believers first called Christians in Antioch. Acts 11:26
Not ashamed to be called a Christian. 1 Peter 4:16

CHRISTMAS
For unto us a child is born. Isa. 9:6
The birth of Jesus. Matt. 1–2; Luke 1–2

CHURCH
The rock on which it's built. Matt. 16:18
Go into all the world. Matt. 28:18–20
The Lord added to it daily. Acts 2:47
One body in Christ. Rom. 12:5
All form one body. 1 Cor. 12:13
Equipped to build it up. Eph. 4:11–12
Christ the head of the church. Eph. 5:23
Do not give up meeting together. Heb. 10:24–25

CIRCUMCISION
Every male circumcised. Gen. 17:10–11
In Christ, it is of no value. Gal. 5:2–11
A matter of the heart. Rom. 2:28–29

CITIZENSHIP
"My people, who are called by my name." 2 Chron. 7:14
Our citizenship is in heaven. Phil. 3:20

CLEAN
God makes us perfectly clean. Ps. 51:7
Be clean inside and out. Matt. 23:25–26
Jesus cleanses us from sin. 1 John 1:7
See also PURITY.

CLOTHING
The first clothing. Gen. 3:7, 21
False prophets wear sheep's clothing. Matt. 7:15
Clothed with the imperishable. 1 Cor. 15:53
Clothed with compassion. Col. 3:12
Wear modest clothing. 1 Tim. 2:9

COMFORT

"Your rod and your staff, they comfort me." Ps. 23:4
God's Word provides comfort. Ps. 119:50
"I will give you rest." Matt. 11:28
Holy Spirit is our Comforter. John 14:16
The God of all comfort. 2 Cor. 1:3

COMMITMENT

"Your God will be my God." Ruth 1:16
God will establish your goals. Prov. 16:3
Take up your cross daily. Luke 9:23
Don't conform to this world. Rom. 12:2
Make effort to grow in faith. 2 Peter 1:5
Choose this day whom you will serve. Josh. 24:15

COMMUNION

"Do this in remembrance of me." Luke 22:19
The breaking of bread. Acts 2:42
Do until Christ returns. 1 Cor. 11:22–26

COMPASSION

God's compassions never fail. Lam. 3:22
Jesus' compassion. Matt. 14:14; Mark 6:34
Be compassionate, humble. 1 Peter 3:8

COMPLAINING

It angered God. Num. 11:1
Do all things without it. Phil. 2:13–14
Don't grumble against others. James 5:9
Show hospitality without it. 1 Peter 4:9

CONDEMNATION

For those of wicked devices. Prov. 12:2
Because of evil deeds. John 3:19
No condemnation in Christ. Rom. 8:1

CONFESSION OF FAITH

"We will serve the Lord." Josh. 24:15
Confess Jesus before others. Matt. 10:32
Declare, "Jesus is Lord." Rom. 10:9–10

CONFESSION OF SIN

Confess your sins to the Lord. Ps. 32:5
Confess sins to one another. James 5:16
God forgives when we confess. 1 John 1:9

CONFIDENCE

God will be your confidence. Prov. 3:26
Preach/teach with confidence. Acts 28:31
Draw near to throne of God. Heb. 4:16

CONFLICT

Hatred stirs it up. Prov. 10:12
Soft answer turns away wrath. Prov. 15:1
Be reconciled to your brother. Matt. 5:24
Live peaceably with all. Rom. 12:18
See also QUARRELING.

CONFUSION

God confused their language. Gen. 11:9
God is not author of confusion. 1 Cor. 14:33
It's where envy and strife are. James 3:16

CONSCIENCE

Strive for a clear conscience. Acts 24:16
A matter of conscience. Rom. 13:5
Our conscience testifies. 2 Cor. 1:12
Good conscience, sincere faith. 1 Tim. 1:5

CONTENTMENT

Neither rich nor poor. Prov. 30:8
Content in whatever state. Phil. 4:11
With godliness, it's great gain. 1 Tim. 6:6
Be content with what you have. Heb. 13:5

A
B
C
D
E
F
G
H
I
J
K
L
M
N
O
P
Q
R
S
T
U
V
W
X
Y
Z

CONVERSION

See Born Again; Salvation.

CONVICTION

They were "cut to the heart." Acts 2:37
Holy Spirit will convict the world about sin. John 16:8
The gospel came with deep conviction. 1 Thess. 1:5

CORNERSTONE

Precious and solid. Isa. 28:16
Christ, the chief cornerstone. Eph. 2:20
Unbelievers rejected it. 1 Peter 2:7

COUNSEL *See* Advice.

COURAGE

Be strong and courageous. Josh. 1:9
Be strong and take heart. Ps. 27:14
Chosen for such a time as this. Est. 4:14
Take heart! Jesus has overcome. John 16:33
Stand firm, be immovable. 1 Cor. 15:58
God gave us a spirit not of fear. 2 Tim. 1:7

COVENANT

God's covenant with Israel. Deut. 30:15–18; 1 Sam. 12:14–15
God remembers his covenant. Ps. 105:8
An everlasting covenant. Jer. 50:5
Old and new covenants. Heb. 8:6
See also New Covenant.

COVETOUSNESS *See* Envy.

CREATION

God created heavens and earth. Gen. 1:1
They worshiped created things. Rom. 1:25
Creation has been groaning. Rom. 8:22
In Christ, a new creation. 2 Cor. 5:17
The firstborn of all creation. Col. 1:15

CREATOR

Remember your Creator. Eccl. 12:1
We are image of our Creator. Col. 3:10
Faithful Creator. 1 Peter 4:19

CRITICAL

Don't judge. Matt. 7:1–5
Say nothing unwholesome. Eph. 4:29
Slandering other believers. James 4:11–12
Put away all slander. 1 Peter 2:1
See also Judging.

CROSS

Take up your cross. Mark 8:34; Luke 9:23
It's foolishness to unbelievers. 1 Cor. 1:18
Glory in the cross. Gal. 6:14
Many are enemies of the cross. Phil. 3:18
Sins nailed to the cross. Col. 2:14–15
The cross endured by Jesus. Heb. 12:2
See also Crucifixion.

CROWN

Crown of thorns. Matt. 27:29
An incorruptible crown. 1 Cor. 9:25
Crown of righteousness. 2 Tim. 4:8
Crown of life. James 1:12
Crown of glory. 1 Peter 5:4
Jesus wears many crowns. Rev. 19:12

CRUCIFIXION

Hands and feet pierced. Ps. 22:16
Shouts for crucifixion. Mark 15:13
Crucified with two thieves. Mark 15:27
Crucified but risen. Acts 4:10
Crucified with Christ. Gal 2:20
See also Cross.

CURSE

Serpent, ground cursed. Gen. 3:14–17
Taking God's name in vain. Ex. 20:7
Christ redeemed us from curse. Gal. 3:13
Will no longer be any curse. Rev. 22:3

CURTAIN

Curtains of the tabernacle. Ex. 26
Temple's curtain torn in two. Matt. 27:51
The curtain, Christ's body. Heb. 10:20

DANCING

David danced before God. 2 Sam. 6:14
Mourning turned into dancing. Ps. 30:11
A time to dance. Eccl. 3:4

DARKNESS

Thrown into outer darkness. Matt 8:12
Light shines in the darkness. John 1:5
Evildoers loved darkness. John 3:19
You were sometimes darkness. Eph. 5:8
In God, there is no darkness. 1 John 1:5

DAUGHTERS *See* CHILDREN.

DAY

God called the light day. Gen. 1:5
The day the Lord has made. Ps. 118:24
Work while it is day. John 9:4
A day is like a thousand years. 2 Peter 3:8

DAY OF THE LORD

It is near. Ezek. 30:3
It is great. Joel 2:11
It will be dark. Amos 5:18
Awesome and incredible. Acts 2:20
It will come as a thief. 2 Peter 3:10

DEACONS

Must be honest. Acts 6:3
Must be blameless. 1 Tim. 3:10

DEAFNESS, SPIRITUAL

Cries will not be heard. Prov. 21:13
Covered ears so not to hear. Zech. 7:11
Are unable to hear. Matt. 13:15
Whoever has ears to hear. Luke 14:35
See also HEARING.

DEATH

From dust to dust. Gen. 3:19; Eccl. 3:20
A way that leads to death. Prov. 14:12
Crossing from death to life. John 5:24
Kernel must die to yield fruit. John 12:24
Wages of sin is death. Rom. 6:23
Death, where is your sting? 1 Cor. 15:55
Appointed for man once to die. Heb. 9:27
Death no more. Rev. 21:4
See also GRAVE.

DEBT

Borrower is slave to lender. Prov. 22:7
Pay all that is owed. Rom. 13:7
Owe only the debt of love. Rom. 13:8

DECEPTION

"Keep me from being deceitful." Ps. 119:29
It conceals hatred. Prov. 26:26
Don't deceive yourself. Gal 6:7
Deceiving oneself. James 1:22

A B C D E F G H I J K L M N O P Q R S T U V W X Y Z

DECISION MAKING

God will direct your path. Prov. 3:5–6
Call and God will answer you. Jer. 33:3
Pray about everything. Phil. 4:6
Ask God for wisdom. James 1:5
See also WILL OF GOD.

DEEDS *See* WORKS.

DEMONS

Jesus cast them out. Matt. 8:28–34
The prince of demons. Matt 12:24
Cast out by prayer and fasting. Mark 9:29
Even the demons believe. James 2:19
Fallen angels. 2 Peter 2:4

DEPRESSION *See* SORROW.

DEVIL *See* SATAN.

DISABILITY

Don't curse the deaf. Lev. 19:14
"I was eyes to the blind and feet to the lame." Job 29:15
Not caused by sin. John 9:3
"My power is made perfect in weakness." 2 Cor. 12:9

DISAPPOINTMENT

Joy will follow weeping. Ps. 30:5
God is with the brokenhearted. Ps 34:18
God has plans for you. Jer. 29:11-14
God will restore you. 1 Peter 5:10

DISCIPLESHIP

Go and make disciples. Matt. 28:18–20
Hold to Jesus' teachings. John 8:31
Carry your cross. Luke 14:27
Disciples known by their love. John 13:35
Followed apostles' teachings. Acts 2:42
Teach what you have learned. 2 Tim. 2:2
See also MENTORING.

DISCIPLINE

God opens ears to discipline. Job 36:10
Shame comes to the undisciplined. Prov. 13:18
To save a child from death. Prov. 23:14
Discipline your children. Eph. 6:4
Train yourself to be godly. 1 Tim. 4:7
God disciplines ones he loves. Heb. 12:6–10
See also REBUKE.

DISCRIMINATION

See FAVORITISM.

DISHONESTY *See* LYING.

DISOBEDIENCE

They disobey their parents. Rom. 1:30
One man's disobedience. Rom. 5:19
God's wrath on disobedience. Eph. 5:6

DIVISION

House divided cannot stand. Matt. 12:25
Avoid those who cause it. Rom. 16:17
Avoid divisions among you. 1 Cor. 1:10
See also UNITY.

DIVORCE

God hates divorce. Mal. 2:16
Don't separate what God has joined together. Matt. 19:1–12
Moses allowed divorce. Mark 10:4–5
If an unbeliever leaves. 1 Cor. 7:11–16

DOCTRINE

Replacing with human rules. Mark 7:7

Carried away by every wind of doctrine. Eph. 4:14
A time when unsound doctrine is desired. 2 Tim. 4:3
See also TEACHERS/TEACHING.

DOMESTIC VIOLENCE
See ABUSE.

DOMINION
Let them have dominion. Gen. 1:26
The upright will rule. Ps. 49:14
Death has none over Jesus. Rom. 6:9
God has dominion forever. Jude 1:25

DOOR
Sin lies at the door. Gen. 4:7
Jesus is the door/gate. John 10:9
Jesus stands and knocks. Rev. 3:20

DOUBT
"You of little faith." Matt. 14:31
"Help my unbelief." Mark 9:24
Doubting Thomas. John 20:24–29
Faith without doubt. James 1:6
Have mercy on doubters. Jude 1:22

DREAMS
God reveals in dreams. Gen. 41:25
Prophesying false dreams. Jer. 23:32
Interpreting dreams. Dan. 4:18
Old men will dream dreams. Acts 2:17
See also VISIONS.

DRUNKENNESS
Drunkards will become poor. Prov. 23:21
Lingering over wine. Prov. 23:29–30
Don't get drunk on wine. Eph. 5:18
See also ADDICTION; ALCOHOL.

DUTY
What the Lord asks of you. Deut. 10:12
Whole duty of mankind. Eccl. 12:13–14
What the Lord requires of you. Mic. 6:8
See also PURPOSE.

EARTH
God created the earth. Gen. 1:1
Earth hangs upon nothing. Job 26:7
Earth is the Lord's. Ps. 24:1
He set earth on its foundation. Ps. 104:5
God enthroned above it. Isa. 40:22

EASTER *See* RESURRECTION.

ELDERLY
Show respect for elders. Lev. 19:32
Don't cast off the elderly. Ps. 71:9
Respect those with gray hair. Prov. 16:31
Honor widows. 1 Tim. 5:3

ELDERS, CHURCH
Commended to God. Acts 14:23
Must be found faithful. 1 Cor. 4:2
Worthy of honor. 1 Tim. 5:17
Must be blameless. Titus 1:6–7

ELECTION
Israel, God's chosen. Isa. 45:4
"I chose you." John 15:16

God's purpose in it. Rom. 9:9–13
Chosen before creation. Eph. 1:4–5
Make sure it is firm. 2 Peter 1:10

ENCOURAGEMENT
Israelites encouraged. Judg. 20:22
God encourages the afflicted. Ps. 10:17
Encourage one another. 1 Thess. 4:18; 5:11

END TIMES
The seventy "sevens." Dan. 9:20–27
Abomination of desolation. Dan. 12:11
Wars and rumors of wars. Matt. 24:6
Great tribulation. Matt. 24:21
God will shorten those days. Matt. 24:22
No one knows the day, hour. Mark 13:32
Terrible times in last days. 2 Tim. 3:1
Mark of the Beast. Rev. 13:17; 14:9, 11; 19:20
Battle of armageddon. Rev. 16:16
See also ANTICHRIST; SECOND COMING.

ENDURANCE
Love endures all things. 1 Cor. 13:7
Jesus endured the cross. Heb. 12:2
God's word endures forever. 1 Peter 1:25
See also PERSEVERANCE.

ENEMIES
God rescues us from enemies. Ps. 18:17
Love your enemies. Matt. 5:44
God will make a footstool of your enemies. Mark 12:36
Many enemies of Christ. Phil. 3:18
A friend of the world is an enemy of God. James 4:4

ENVY
"You shall not covet." Ex. 20:17
Envy makes the bones rot. Prov. 14:30
Don't envy the wicked. Prov. 23:17; 24:1
Love does not envy. 1 Cor. 13:4
Envy and selfish ambition. James 3:16
See also JEALOUSY.

ETERNAL LIFE
Eternity in our hearts. Eccl. 3:11
The road that leads to life. Matt. 17:13–14
Believers will not perish. John 3:16
Believers have eternal life. John 5:24
This is eternal life. John 17:3
It is the free gift of God. Rom. 6:23
Sow in Spirit; reap eternal life. Gal. 6:8
See also LIFE.

EUCHARIST *See* COMMUNION.

EVANGELISM
The harvest is ripe. Matt. 9:37
Go into all the world. Mark 16:15
Gift of evangelism. Eph. 4:11
Always be ready to answer. 1 Peter 3:15
See also MISSIONS; WITNESSES.

EVIL
"I will fear no evil." Ps. 23:4
God will judge every act. Eccl. 12:14
Reject every kind of evil. 1 Thess. 5:22
Untamed tongue is evil. James 3:6–8
Repay evil with blessing. 1 Peter 3:9

EYES
An eye for an eye. Deut. 19:21; Matt. 5:38–39
The apple of God's eye. Ps. 17:8 ; Zech. 2:8
If your eye causes you to sin. Matt. 5:29
The eye is the lamp of the body. Matt. 6:22; Luke 11:34
Take speck out of your own eye. Luke 6:42
See also BLINDNESS; SIGHT.

FACE
Can't see God's face and live. Ex. 33:20
"Make your face shine upon us." Ps. 80:3
Then we'll see face to face. 1 Cor. 13:12

FAILURES
Though the heart fails, God is its strength. Ps. 73:26
Righteous fall, get back up. Prov. 24:16
Spirit is willing, flesh is weak. Matt. 26:41
Forget the past, look to future. Phil. 3:14

FAITH
The just shall live by faith. Hab. 2:4
Faith as a mustard seed. Matt. 17:20
Faith comes from hearing. Rom. 10:17
Walk by faith. 2 Cor. 5:7
Saved through faith. Eph. 2:8–9
Substance of things hoped for. Heb. 11:1
Without faith, it is impossible to please God. Heb. 11:6
Author and finisher of faith. Heb. 12:2

FAITHFULNESS
To all generations. Ps. 89:1
New each morning. Lam. 3:23
Good and faithful servant. Matt. 25:23
God is Faithful and True. Rev. 19:11
See also LOYALTY.

FALL OF MANKIND
Adam, Eve, and the serpent. Gen. 3
Sin entered the world. Rom. 5:12
See also ORIGINAL SIN.

FALSE GODS
Get rid of other gods. Gen. 35:2
Shall have no other gods. Ex. 20:3
Made God angry and jealous. Deut. 32:16
No salvation in other gods. Acts 4:12
See also IDOLATRY; MONOTHEISM.

FALSE TEACHERS
Danger of presuming to speak. Deut. 18:20
Wolves in sheep's clothing. Matt. 7:15
Give unsound instruction. 1 Tim. 6:3
Soothe itching ears. 2 Tim. 4:3
They will be among you. 2 Peter 2:1

FAMILY
Honor father and mother. Ex. 20:12
"As for me and my household, we will serve the Lord." Josh. 24:15
Train children. Prov. 13:24; 22:6; 23:13
Provide for your family. 1 Tim. 5:8
The family of believers. 1 Peter 2:17
See also CHILDREN; FATHERS; MOTHERS; MARRIAGE.

FAMINE
Famine of hearing God's words. Amos 8:11
Famines in last days. Matt. 24:7; Luke 21:11

FARMING
Food from the earth. Gen. 1:29
Praise God for good land. Deut. 8:10
Seed in good ground yields fruit. Matt. 13:8
Farmer waits for the crop. James 5:7
See also HARVEST; SEEDS.

FASTING
We don't live on bread alone. Deut. 8:3
Daniel's fasts. Dan. 1:12–13; 10:3
Jesus' fast in the wilderness. Matt. 4:2
Not like the hypocrites. Matt. 6:16

FATHERHOOD OF GOD
God is a father to all. Ps. 68:5
The one Father, in heaven. Matt. 23:9
Our Father in heaven. Luke 11:2
We cry "Abba, Father." Rom. 8:15
Father of lights. James 1:17

FATHERS
Honor father and mother. Ex. 20:12
Teach children commandments. Deut. 6:7
Don't provoke children to anger. Eph. 6:4; Col. 3:21
Discipline their children. Heb. 12:9
See also FAMILY.

FAVORITISM
God doesn't play favorites. Acts 10:34; Rom. 2:11; Gal. 2:6; Eph. 6:9
All are one in Christ. Gal. 3:28
Do not show favoritism. James 2:1, 9

FEAR
"I will fear no evil." Ps. 23:4
God is in control. Ps. 46:10
"Fear not. For I am with you." Isa. 41:10
Don't fear humans. Matt. 10:28
Don't be afraid, keep speaking. Acts 18:9
We don't have a spirit of fear. 2 Tim. 1:7
Perfect love casts out fear. 1 John 4:18

FEAR OF THE LORD
Act with reverence. Neh. 5:15
The wicked have none. Ps. 36:1
The beginning of knowledge. Prov. 1:7
Perfecting holiness. 2 Cor. 7:1

FEASTS/FESTIVALS
First Passover. Ex. 12
Pentecost/Feast of Weeks. Ex. 34:22; Acts 2
Day of Atonement/Yom Kippur. Lev. 16
Seven appointed feasts. Lev. 23
Feast of Lots/Purim. Est. 9:20–32

FELLOWSHIP
A cord of three not broken. Eccl. 4:9–12
A gathering of two or three. Matt. 18:20
Fellowship with Jesus. 1 Cor. 1:9
Continue to meet together. Heb. 10:24–25
Fellowship with one another. 1 John 1:7

FINANCES *See* MONEY.

FIRE
God is a consuming fire. Deut. 4:24
God's word is like a fire. Jer. 23:29
Refined by fire. Zech. 13:9; 1 Peter 1:7
Baptized with fire. Matt. 3:11
Tongues of fire. Acts 2:3
The tongue is a fire. James 3:6
The lake of fire. Rev. 19:20; 20:10–15

FIRSTBORN
Firstborn among many. Rom. 8:29
Firstborn over every creature. Col. 1:15
Firstborn from the dead. Col. 1:18
Church of the firstborn. Heb. 12:23

FIRSTFRUITS
Bring it into God's house. Ex. 23:19
Honor God with firstfruits. Prov. 3:9
Firstfruits of the spirit. Rom. 8:23
Firstfruits of the dead. 1 Cor. 15:20

FISH

God created fish of the sea. Gen. 1:20
Fishers of men. Matt. 4:19
God's kingdom like a fishnet. Matt. 13:47
Miracle of fish and loaves. Matt. 14:13–21

FLATTERY

Deceptive lips. Ps. 12:2
Rebuke is better than flattery. Prov. 28:23
Flattery is a trap. Prov. 29:5

FLESH

Spirit willing but flesh weak. Mark 14:38
Flesh vs. Spirit. Rom. 8:5–12
It lusts against the Spirit. Gal. 5:17
We don't wrestle against flesh and blood. Eph. 6:12
Lust of the flesh. 1 John 2:16

FLOOD, THE

Noah, the ark, and the flood. Gen. 6–9

FLOWERS

Rose of Sharon. Song 2:1
Grass withers, flower fades. Isa. 40:8
Lilies of the field. Matt. 6:28

FOLLOWING JESUS

Take up your cross and follow Jesus. Matt. 16:24; Mark 8:34
Will not walk in darkness. John 8:12
Follow in Jesus' steps. 1 Peter 2:21
Walk as Jesus walked. 1 John 2:6
See also Discipleship.

FOOD

Eat, drink, be merry. Eccl. 8:15; Luke 12:19
Eat your food joyfully. Eccl. 9:7
"You prepare a table before me." Ps. 23:5
Do all for God's glory. 1 Cor. 10:31
See also Bread; Fasting.

FOOLS/FOOLISHNESS

Fools despise wisdom. Prov. 1:7
Saying, "You fool!" Matt. 5:22
Gospel is foolishness to some. 1 Cor. 1:18
Foolish wisdom of this world. 1 Cor. 3:19
Fools for Christ. 1 Cor. 4:10

FOOT WASHING

Jesus' feet washed with tears. Luke 7:44
Jesus washed disciples' feet. John 13:5

FOREIGNERS

Love foreigners as yourself. Lev. 19:34
Foreigners no longer. Eph. 2:12, 19

FORGIVENESS

Love covers all sins. Prov. 10:12
Forgive others. Matt. 6:15
Forgive seventy times seven. Matt. 18:22
Forgive us our sins. Luke 11:4
"Father, forgive them." Luke 23:34
Confession and forgiveness. 1 John 1:9

FORSAKEN

"My God, my God, why have you forsaken me?" Ps. 22:1; Mark 15:34
The righteous never forsaken. Ps. 37:25
God will always be with you. Heb. 13:5

FREEDOM

Truth will set you free. John 8:32
The Son frees you. John 8:36
Free from sin. Rom. 6:18
Where the Spirit of the Lord is, there is freedom. 2 Cor. 3:17
Not freedom to indulge flesh. Gal. 5:13

FRIENDSHIP

Choose friends carefully. Prov 12:26
A friend loves at all times. Prov. 17:17
Sticks closer than a brother. Prov. 18:24
As iron sharpens iron. Prov. 27:17
Two is better than one. Eccl. 4:9–12
Lay down his life for friends. John 15:13

FRUIT

Bear fruit of repentance. Matt. 3:8
A tree is recognized by its fruit. Matt. 7:15–16; Luke 6:44
Fruit of the Spirit Gal. 5:22–23

GAMBLING

See Addiction; Money.

GATES

Narrow gate that leads to life. Matt. 7:14
Hades' gates won't prevail. Matt. 16:18
The sheep gate. John 10:1–10
The pearly gates. Rev. 21:21

GENEROSITY

Give generously to the poor. Deut. 15:10
The generous will prosper. Prov. 11:25
Generosity in sharing. 2 Cor. 9:13
God is generous. James 1:5
See also Giving.

GENTILES

A light to the Gentiles. Isa. 49:6
Salvation sent to Gentiles. Acts 28:28
Paul, apostle to Gentiles. Rom. 11:13
Gentiles grafted in. Rom. 11:17–18

GENTLENESS

Gentleness of Jesus. Matt. 11:29
A fruit of the Spirit. Gal. 5:23
Restore someone gently. Gal. 6:1
Answer gently. 1 Peter 3:15

GIFTS

Father gives good gifts. Luke 11:11–13
The gift of the Holy Spirit. Acts 2:38
God's indescribable gift! 2 Cor. 9:15
Eternal life, the gift of God. Eph. 2:8
Every good gift is from God. James 1:17
Gifts to serve others. 1 Peter 4:10
See also Spiritual Gifts.

GIVING

Lord gives and Lord takes away. Job 1:21
Give to anyone who asks. Luke 6:30–38
More blessed to give than receive. Acts 20:35
God loves a cheerful giver. 2 Cor. 9:7
See also Generosity; Tithes.

GLORY

God's glory filled tabernacle. Ex. 40:34
Earth is full of God's glory. Isa. 6:3
We've seen the Son's glory. John 1:14
All fall short of God's glory. Rom. 3:23
Glorify God in everything. 1 Cor. 10:31
Changed from glory to glory. 2 Cor. 3:18

GLUTTONY

Gluttons will become poor. Prov. 23:21
Serve God, not appetites. Rom. 16:18

GOD

All-Knowing (Omniscient)
Nothing is hidden from God. Heb. 4:13

All-Places (Omnipresent)
God's presence always. Ps. 139:7–12

All-Powerful (Omnipotent)
Nothing is too hard for God. Jer. 32:17
With God, all is possible. Matt. 19:26

Eternal
From everlasting to everlasting. Ps. 90:2
The everlasting God. Isa. 40:28

Good
The Lord is good. Ps. 145:9; Nah. 1:7

Holy
Be holy because God is holy. Lev. 19:2
Holy, holy, holy is the Lord. Isa. 6:3

Immutable (Doesn't Change)
"I, the Lord, do not change." Mal. 3:6

Just Judge
Judge the world in righteousness. Ps. 9:8
The Lord is our judge. Isa. 33:22

Creator
In the beginning God created. Gen. 1:1
We are sheep of his pasture. Ps. 100:3
Hairs on your head numbered. Luke 12:6–7

Loving
Compassionate and gracious. Ex. 34:6–7
Wonderfully made by God. Ps. 139:13–16
God is love. 1 John 4:8

One God
The Lord our God is one. Deut. 6:4
"Apart from me there is no God."
Isa. 44:6; 45:5–6

NAMES OF GOD

Adonai .... Isa. 40:3–5
Meaning: My great Lord
El Elyon .... Ps. 78:35
Meaning: God most high
Elohim .... Deut. 10:17
Meaning: All-powerful one
El Olam .... Gen. 21:33
Meaning: Eternal God
El Roi .... Ps. 139:7–12
Meaning: God who sees me
El Shaddai .... Gen. 35:11
Meaning: All-sufficient one
Immanuel .... Isa. 7:14; 8:8–10
Meaning: God with us
Jehovah/Yahweh .... Ex. 3:14
Meaning: "I AM"; The one who is
Jehovah-Jireh .... Gen. 22:14
Meaning: Lord will provide
Jehovah-Rapha .... Ex. 15:26
Meaning: Lord who heals
Jehovah-Rohi .... Ps. 23:1
Meaning: Lord is my shepherd
Jehovah-Shalom .... Judg. 6:24
Meaning: Lord is peace

GOLDEN RULE
Do unto others. Matt. 7:12; Luke 6:31

GOOD SAMARITAN
Parable of the neighbor. Luke 10:25–37

GOOD SHEPHERD
"I am the good shepherd." John 10:11–14

GOODNESS
God intended it for good. Gen. 50:20

"Goodness will follow me." Ps. 23:6
Taste and see, the Lord is good. Ps. 34:8
God works all for the good. Rom. 8:28
A fruit of the Spirit. Gal. 5:22
Desire goodness. 2 Thess. 1:11

GOSPEL/GOOD NEWS

Those who bring good news. Isa. 52:7
Will be preached all over world. Matt 24:14
Believe the good news. Mark 1:15
Anointed to preach good news. Luke 4:18
Not ashamed of the gospel. Rom. 1:16
Saved by the gospel. 1 Cor. 15:1–4
A different gospel. Gal. 1:6–9

GOSSIP

A whisperer separates friends. Prov. 16:28
Their words are wounds. Prov. 18:8
Empty words. Matt. 12:36
Corrupt words. Eph. 4:29
Busybodies. 2 Thess. 3:11
Avoid godless babblings. 2 Tim. 2:16

GOVERNMENT

Shall be on Christ's shoulders. Isa. 9:6
Obey God above men. Acts 5:29
Subject to those who govern. Rom. 13:1–5
See also AUTHORITY.

GRACE

God has shown grace. Ezra 9:8
Given to the humble. Prov. 3:34; 1 Peter 5:5
Not under law, but grace. Rom. 6:14
God's grace is sufficient. 2 Cor. 12:9
God's free gift. Eph. 2:8–9
God's throne of grace. Heb. 4:16

GRANDCHILDREN

Crown of their grandparents. Prov. 17:6

GRAVE

God will deliver us from it. Hos. 13:14
Those in graves will hear God. John 5:28
Lazarus called out of it. John 12:17
See also DEATH; HADES.

GREAT COMMISSION

Go and teach all people. Matt. 28:19–20

GREATNESS

God has shown us his greatness. Deut. 5:24
Great is the Lord. Ps. 48:1; 145:3; 150:2
He must become greater. John 3:30
Greater is he who is in you. 1 John 4:4

GREED

It troubles one's own house. Prov. 15:27
Lovers of money never have enough. Eccl. 5:10
They're out for their own gain. Isa. 56:11
Guard against greed. Luke 12:15
See also ENVY; MONEY.

GRIEF

Turned mourning into dancing. Ps. 30:11
Christ would know grief. Isa. 53:3–4
Mourners will be comforted. Matt. 5:4
Mourn with those who mourn. Rom. 12:15
Don't grieve like those without hope. 1 Thess. 4:13
There will be no more grief. Rev. 21:4
See also TEARS; WEEPING.

GRUDGES

Don't bear a grudge. Lev. 19:19
Love keeps no record of wrongs. 1 Cor. 13:5
See also BITTERNESS.

GRUMBLING *See* COMPLAINING.

GUIDANCE

God's word is a light. Ps. 119:105
Do not lean on your own understanding. Prov. 3:5
God will direct your path. Prov. 3:6
Holy Spirit will guide you. John 16:13
Ask God for wisdom. James 1:5
See also Advice; Will of God.

GUILT

Guilt is taken away. Isa. 6:7
As far as east is from west, God has removed transgressions. Ps. 103:12
No guilt found in Jesus. John 18:38
Failure in one point of the law is to be guilty of all. James 2:10
See also Condemnation.

HABITS

Do all to the glory of God. 1 Cor. 10:31
Show yourself able to handle the gospel. 2 Tim. 2:15
Continue to meet together. Heb. 10:25

HADES

Its gates will not overcome. Matt. 16:18
Keys of death and Hades. Rev. 1:18
Thrown into the lake of fire. Rev. 20:14
See also Grave; Hell.

HAIR

Are all numbered. Matt. 10:30
Wiped Jesus' feet with her hair. Luke 7:38
Long hair is a covering. 1 Cor. 11:15

HALLELUJAH

A great roar in heaven. Rev. 19:1–6
See also Praise; Worship.

HANDS

Lift your hands in praise. Ps. 134:2
No one can snatch you out of the Father's hand. John 10:29
Laid hands upon. Mark 10:16; Luke 4:40; Acts 8:17; Acts 13:3
God's mighty hand. 1 Peter 5:6

HAPPINESS

Delight in God. Ps. 37:4
A happy heart. Prov. 15:13
Rejoice in the Lord always. Phil. 4:4
See also Cheerful; Joy.

HARDSHIP

See Suffering; Trials.

HARMONY

Live in harmony. Rom. 12:16
Have Christ's attitude. Rom. 15:5
Love binds everything together. Col. 3:14
See also Unity.

HARVEST

Leave some for the poor. Lev. 23:22
Pray to the Lord of harvest. Matt. 9:38
It is great, but the workers few. Luke 10:2
The fields are ripe. John 4:35
You will reap what you sow. Gal. 6:7
See also Farming; Seeds.

HATRED

Hatred stirs up strife. Prov. 10:12
Do good to those who hate you. Matt. 5:44
If the world hates you. John 15:18
No one ever hated his own flesh. Eph. 5:29
Don't be surprised by the world's hatred of you. 1 John 3:13

HEAD

Coals on your enemy's head. Rom. 12:20
Head coverings in worship. 1 Cor. 11:2–16
Jesus, the head of the church. Col. 1:18

HEALING

God will heal the land. 2 Chron. 7:14
Heals the brokenhearted. Ps. 147:3
By Jesus' stripes we are healed. Isa. 53:5
Healing in his wings. Mal. 4:2
"Physician, heal yourself." Luke 4:23
Just say the word. Luke 7:7
See also ILLNESS.

HEARING

Hear, O Israel. Deut. 6:4–5
Samuel called and answered. 1 Sam. 3:4
He that has ears, let him hear. Matt. 11:15
Practice what you hear. Luke 8:21
Faith comes by hearing. Rom. 10:17
We know that he hears us. 1 John 5:15
"I stand at the door and knock." Rev. 3:20
See also DEAFNESS, SPIRITUAL.

HEART

God looks at the heart. 1 Sam. 16:7
Ask for a pure heart. Ps. 51:10.
Guard your heart. Prov. 4:23
Deceitful above all things. Jer. 17:9
Where your treasure is. Luke 12:34
Let it not be troubled. John 14:1
With it, you believe. Rom. 10:10
Thoughts and intents of it. Heb. 4:12

HEAVEN

A voice from heaven. Matt. 3:17
Treasures in heaven. Matt. 6:20
God will come down. 1 Thess. 4:16
A new heaven and a new earth. Rev. 21:1

HELL

In danger of hellfire. Matt. 5:22
Weeping and gnashing of teeth. Matt. 13:50
Gates will not prevail. Matt. 16:18
Lake of Fire. Rev. 20:14–15
See also HADES.

HELP

A suitable helper for man. Gen. 2:18
Where does help come from? Ps. 121:1
Help in time of need. Heb. 4:16
The Lord is our helper. Heb. 13:6

HERESY

Preaching another Jesus. 2 Cor. 11:4
A different gospel. Gal. 1:6–8
Destructive heresies. 2 Peter 2:1
See also FALSE TEACHERS.

HOLINESS

The beauty of his holiness. Ps. 29:2
Holy, holy, holy is the Lord. Isa. 6:3; Rev 4:8
Spirit of holiness. Rom. 1:4
Called to a holy life. 2 Tim. 1:9
Holiness to see God. Heb. 12:14
Be holy because God is. 1 Peter 1:15–16

HOLY OF HOLIES

See MOST HOLY PLACE.

HOLY SPIRIT

Guides

Our counselor/advocate. John 14:16
Teaches us all things. John 14:26
Guides us into all truth. John 16:13

Empowers

Believers receive power. Acts 1:8
Disciples filled, speak in tongues. Acts 2:4
Different gifts, same Spirit. 1 Cor. 12:4–13
Strengthens believers. Eph. 3:16

Lives in Believers

Intercedes with groans. Rom. 8:26
Body is temple of Holy Spirit. 1 Cor. 6:19
Gives gifts to believers. 1 Cor. 12, 14; Eph. 4
Spirit calls out, "Abba, Father." Gal. 4:6
Spirit is a seal and deposit. Eph. 1:13–14

NAMES OF HOLY SPIRIT

Advocate/Comforter	John 14:16; 15:26
Eternal Spirit	Heb. 9:14
Good Spirit	Neh. 9:20; Ps. 143:10
Holy Spirit	Ps. 51:11; Luke 11:13
Power of the Highest	Luke 1:35
Spirit of Adoption	Rom. 8:15
Spirit of Burning	Isa. 4:4
Spirit of Christ	Rom. 8:9; 1 Peter 1:11
Spirit of Glory	1 Peter 4:14
Spirit of Grace	Zech. 12:10; Heb. 10:29
Spirit of Judgment	Isa. 28:6
Spirit of Knowledge	Isa. 11:2
Spirit of Life	Rom. 8:2
Spirit of the Living God	2 Cor. 3:3
Spirit of Prophecy	Rev. 19:10
Spirit of Truth	John 14:17; 15:26
Spirit of Wisdom	Eph. 1:7

HOMOSEXUALITY

Forbidden. Lev. 18:22
Unnatural sexual relations. Rom. 1:26–27
Will not inherit the kingdom. 1 Cor. 6:9

HONESTY

An honest answer. Prov. 24:26
Let us walk honestly. Rom. 13:13
Do what is honest. 2 Cor. 13:7
See also LYING; SINCERITY.

HONOR

Honor your father and mother. Deut. 5:16
Church elders are worthy of double honor. 1 Tim. 5:17
Honor all people. 1 Peter 2:17
Honor your wife. 1 Peter 3:7
God is worthy to receive honor. Rev. 4:11

HOPE

"My hope is in you." Ps. 39:7
Hope in God renews strength. Isa. 40:31
Blessed by hope in God. Jer. 17:7
Faith, hope, charity remain. 1 Cor. 13:13
Having no hope. Eph. 2:12
Christ in you, the hope of glory. Col. 1:27
The blessed hope. Titus 2:13
Anchor of hope. Heb. 6:19

HOSANNA

Hosanna in the highest. Matt. 21:9
To the son of David. Matt. 21:15
To he who comes in the name of the Lord. Mark 11:9
To the king of Israel. John 12:13
See also PRAISE.

HOSPITALITY

Hospitality to strangers. Lev. 19:34

A B C D E F G H I J K L M N O P Q R S T U V W X Y Z

Practice hospitality. Rom. 12:13
A lover of hospitality. Titus 1:8
To strangers, angels unaware. Heb. 13:2
Do it without grumbling. 1 Peter 4:9

HOUSE

"As for me and my household, we will serve the Lord." Josh. 24:15
Dwell in the house of the Lord. Ps. 23:6
Built a house on a rock. Matt. 7:24
House divided cannot stand. Matt. 12:25
"In my Father's house are many mansions." John 14:2
Home in body, away from God. 2 Cor. 5:6

HUMANITY

Created in God's image. Gen. 1:26–27
Fearfully and wonderfully made. Ps. 139:14

HUMBLE/HUMILITY

Humility before honor. Prov. 15:33; 18:12
Jesus is humble in heart. Matt. 11:29
Humble will be glorified. Luke 18:14
Serving Lord with humility. Acts 20:19
God favors the humble. James 4:6
Clothed with humility. 1 Peter 5:5

HUNGER

An idle soul suffers hunger. Prov. 19:15
Hunger for righteousness. Matt. 5:6
Feed your enemy. Rom. 12:20
There will be no more hunger. Rev. 7:16

HUSBANDS

Your maker is your husband. Isa. 54:5
Unbelieving husband is sanctified by a believing wife. 1 Cor. 7:14
Love your wives. Eph. 5:25; Col 3:19
Honor your wife. 1 Peter 3:7

HYPOCRISY/HYPOCRITES

Destroys his neighbor. Prov. 11:9
Don't be as they are. Matt. 6:5
Like whitewashed tombs! Matt. 23:27
The leaven of the Pharisees. Luke 12:1
Rid yourself of hypocrisy. 1 Peter 2:1

IDENTITY IN CHRIST

BELIEVERS IN JESUS ARE:

Accepted .... Rom. 15:7
Born Again .... John 3:3–7
Children of God .... 1 John 3:1–2
Chosen .... 2 Thess. 2:13
Citizens of Heaven .... Phil. 3:20
Empowered .... Eph. 6:10–17
Forgiven .... Col. 2:13
Friends of Jesus .... John 15:15
Lights in the World .... Matt. 5:14–16
Loved .... 1 John 4:10
Ministers .... 2 Cor. 5:18
New Creations .... 2 Cor. 5:17
Royal Priesthood .... 1 Peter 2:9
Temple of Holy Spirit .... 1 Cor. 6:19
Redeemed .... 1 Peter 1:18–19
Saints .... Rom. 1:7
Saved .... Acts 16:30–31
Servants of God .... 2 Cor. 6:4
Soldiers of Christ .... 2 Tim. 2:3

IDOLATRY

No graven images. Ex. 20:4
Do not turn to idols. Lev. 19:4
Graven images destroyed. Mic. 1:7
Flee from idolatry. Gal. 5:20
Idolatry is covetousness. Col. 3:5
See also FALSE GODS.

IGNORANCE

God won't disregard it. Acts 17:30
Doing good silences ignorant talk. 1 Peter 2:15

ILLNESS

Fix your eyes on the eternal. 2 Cor. 4:16–19
God's power in weakness. 2 Cor. 12:9
Elders pray, anoint the sick. James 5:14–15
See also HEALING.

IMAGE OF GOD

Created in God's image. Gen. 1:26–27
Changed into the same image. 2 Cor. 3:18
Christ, the image of God. 2 Cor. 4:4
Image of the invisible God. Col. 1:15

IMITATE

Imitators of Christ. 1 Cor. 11:1
Imitators of God. Eph. 5:1
Follow in Jesus' steps. 1 Peter 2:21
Don't imitate evil. 3 John 1:11

IMMATURITY

Fed with milk, not meat. 1 Cor. 3:2
No longer be children. Eph. 4:14
You need to be taught again. Heb. 5:12
See also SPIRITUAL GROWTH.

IMMORALITY

It leads to the grave. Prov. 7:27
Do not associate with it. 1 Cor. 5:9
No inheritance for the immoral. Eph. 5:5
Abstain from it. 1 Thess. 4:3
See also SEXUAL IMMORALITY.

INHERITANCE

Leave inheritance for children. Prov. 13:22
Sharers in the holy inheritance. Col. 1:12
Inheritance in the Lord. Col. 3:24
One that will never perish. 1 Peter 1:4

INNOCENCE

Be innocent as doves. Matt. 10:16
Be innocent about evil. Rom. 16:19
A clear conscience doesn't mean innocence. 1 Cor. 4:4

INSTRUCTION

Fools despise instruction. Prov. 1:7
A wise son listens to his father. Prov. 13:1
Instruct children in the Lord. Eph. 6:4
Scripture is profitable for it. 2 Tim. 3:16
See also LEARNING; TEACHING.

INTEGRITY

Integrity guides the upright. Prov. 11:3
Show integrity. Titus 2:7

INTERCESSION

Intercession for transgressors. Isa. 53:12
Spirit intercedes for us. Rom. 8:27
Jesus intercedes for us. Rom. 8:34; Heb. 7:25
See also MEDIATOR.

ISRAEL

God's people. 2 Sam. 7:23
The Holy One of Israel. Isa. 49:7
Will never again be uprooted. Amos 9:15
Israel will be saved. Rom. 9:25; 11:26

A B C D E F G H I J K L M N O P Q R S T U V W X Y Z

JEALOUSY

God is a jealous God. Ex. 34:14; Deut. 5:9
Who can stand before it? Prov. 27:4
Jealousy, a work of the flesh. Gal. 5:21
A godly jealousy. 2 Cor. 11:2
See also ENVY.

JESUS

The Son of God

Beloved Son of God. Matt. 3:17
Son of the living God. Matt. 16:16
Only begotten Son. John 3:16

Savior

Came seek and save the lost. Luke 19:10
He gives life to the full. John 10:10
The resurrection and life. John 11:25–26
The way, truth, and life. John 14:6
Salvation found in no one else. Acts 4:12
The one mediator. 1 Tim. 2:5

Loving Lord

How deep is Christ's love! Eph. 3:18
Every knee bow, every tongue confess that Jesus is Lord. Phil. 2:10–11

Coming Again

Coming in clouds with glory. Mark 13:26
He will take us to heaven with him. John 14:2–3

NAMES OF JESUS

Alpha and Omega	Rev. 1:8
Author and Finisher	Heb. 12:2
Branch	Isa. 11:1
Bread of Life	John 6:32–35
Bridegroom	Matt. 9:15
Cornerstone	1 Peter 2:6
Door	John 10:9
Firstborn	Heb. 3:1–2
Good Shepherd	John 10:7–14
Head of Church	Eph. 5:23
High Priest	Heb. 12:23
Immanuel	Matt. 1:23
Judge	John 5:22
King of Kings	Rev. 17:14
Lamb of God	John 1:29
Light of the World	John 8:12
Lion of Judah	Rev. 5:5
Living Water	John 4:10; 7:38
Lord of Lords	Rev. 19:16
Messiah (Christ)	John 1:41; 4:25
Prince of Peace	Isa. 9:6
Redeemer	Job 19:25
Resurrection and Life	John 11:25
Vine	John 15:1
Wonderful Counselor	Isa. 9:6
Word	John 1:1–14

Human and Divine

The Word made flesh. John 1:14
Jesus made the Father known. John 1:18
"Before Abraham was, I am." John 8:58
"I and the Father are one." John 10:30
Thomas said, "My Lord and my God!" John 20:28
Fullness of deity in bodily form. Col. 2:9
Fully human in every way. Heb. 2:17

LIFE OF JESUS

EVENT	MATT.	MARK	LUKE	JOHN
Genealogy	1:1–17		3:23–38	
Annunciation			1:26–38	
Birth in Bethlehem	2:4–6		2:1–20	
Magi visit	2:1–12			
In the temple (age 12)			2:40–52	
Begins ministry (age 30)		1:1	3:1–2	
Baptized	3:3–17	1:9–11	3:21–23	
Wilderness temptation	4:1–11	1:12–13	4:1–13	
Calls first disciples	4:18–22	1:16–20		
Changes water into wine				2:1–11
First cleansing of temple				2:13–22
Samaritan woman at the well				4:5–26
Heals man with leprosy	8:2–4	1:40–45	5:12–16	
Heals paralyzed man	9:1–8	2:1–12	5:17–26	
Sermon on the Mount/ Beatitudes	5:1–7:29			
Lord's Prayer	6:9–13	11:1–4		
Heals a centurion's servant	8:5–13		7:1–10	
Calms a storm	8:23–27	4:35–41	8:22–25	
Raises girl from dead and heals woman with an illness	9:18–26	5:21–43	8:40–56	
Miracle of loaves and fishes	14:15–21	6:35–44	9:12–17	6:4–13
Walks on water	14:24–33	6:47–52		6:16–21
Identified as Messiah	16:13–20	8:27–30	9:18–20	
Predicts his death and resurrection	16:21–26	8:31–37	9:22–25	

EVENT	MATT.	MARK	LUKE	JOHN
Transfiguration	17:1–8	9:2–8	9:28–36	
Casts out demons	17:14–20	9:14–29	9:37–43	
Heals man born blind				9:1–41
Raises Lazarus from the dead				11:1–44
Heals blind Bartimaeus	20:29–34	10:46–52	18:35–43	
Feet anointed by Mary	26:6–13	14:3–9		11:55–12:11
Triumphal Entry/Palm Sunday	21:1–11	11:1–11	19:29–44	12:12–19
Second cleansing of temple	21:12–13	11:15–18	19:45–48	
Olivet Discourse	24:1–25	13:1–37	21:5–36	
Last Supper	26:17–30	14:12–26	22:7–20	13:1–14:31
Washes disciples' feet				13:1–17
Garden of Gethsemane	26:36–46	14:32–42	22:39–46	18:1
Betrayed by Judas	26:47–56	14:43–52	22:47–53	18:2–12
Put on trial; denied by Peter	26:57–27:14	14:53–15:5	22:54–23:5	18:15–38
Sentenced by Pilate	27:15–26	15:6–15	23:13–25	18:39–19:16
Beaten, mocked, crucified	27:27–44	15:16–32	23:26–43	19:18–27
Death on the cross	27:45–56	15:33–41	23:44–49	19:28–37
Buried in tomb	27:57–66	15:42–47	23:50–56	19:38–42
Resurrection	28:1–8	16:1–8	24:1–11	20:1–10
Appears to Mary Magdalene				20:11–18
On the road to Emmaus			24:13–32	
Appears to disciples	28:16–20		24:36–49	20:19–21:14
Restores Peter				21:15–25
Great Commission	28:16–20			
Ascension to heaven		16:19–20	24:50–53 (Acts 1:1–11)	

JEWS

A holy people to God. Deut. 7:6
Jesus, King of the Jews. Luke 23:38
First to the Jew; then Gentile. Rom. 1:16
Neither Jew nor Gentile; all are heirs in Christ. Gal. 3:28
See also ISRAEL.

JOY

There was joy in Israel. 1 Chron. 12:40
Make a joyful noise. Ps. 81:1
Joy over those who repent. Luke 15:10
Your joy may be complete. John 15:11
A fruit of the Spirit. Gal. 5:22
Jesus endured the cross for the joy set before him. Heb. 12:2
Count it all joy. James 1:2
See also CHEERFUL; HAPPINESS.

JUDGING

God, the judge of the earth. Gen. 18:25
God sent judges. Judg. 2:16
Judge righteously. Prov. 31:9
Do not judge others. Matt. 7:1–5
The Son will judge. John 5:22
Stop judging by appearances. John 7:24
Jesus did not come to judge but to save the world. John 12:47
The Spirit-filled person makes judgments. 1 Cor. 2:15
Living and dead will be judged. 1 Peter 4:5
God judges in righteousness. Rev. 19:11

JUDGMENT DAY

Everyone will give account. Matt. 12:36
Will separate sheep from goats. Matt. 25:32
The judgment seat. 2 Cor. 5:10
See also WRATH OF GOD.

JUSTICE

Do no injustice in court. Lev. 19:15
Give justice to the afflicted. Ps. 82:3
Seek justice, defend oppressed. Isa. 1:17
"I the Lord love justice." Isa. 61:8
Let justice roll like a river. Amos 5:24
Act justly, love mercy. Mic. 6:8
Justice for the elect. Luke 18:7–8
See also PUNISHMENT.

JUSTIFICATION

All who believe are justified. Acts 13:39
Raised for our justification. Rom. 4:25
One act of righteousness led to justification. Rom. 5:18
Justified by faith. Gal. 3:24
Justified by God's grace. Titus 3:7

KEYS

Keys of the house of David. Isa. 22:22
Keys of kingdom of heaven. Matt. 16:19
Keys of knowledge. Luke 11:52
Keys of hell and death. Rev. 1:18
Key of David. Rev. 3:7
Key to the bottomless pit. Rev. 9:1

KINDNESS

Brings benefit to yourself. Prov. 11:17
God's lovingkindness. Jonah 4:2

Love is kind. 1 Cor. 13:4
A fruit of the Spirit. Gal. 5:22–23
Be kind to one another. Eph. 4:32
Clothe yourself with it. Col. 3:12
Kindness of our God. Titus 3:4

KINGDOM OF GOD

Your kingdom come. Matt. 6:10; Luke 11:2
Seek it first. Matt. 6:33; Luke 12:31
Easier for a camel through an eye of a needle than rich to enter. Matt. 19:24
The keys of the kingdom. Matt. 16:19
Kingdom is at hand. Mark 1:15
Proclaim the kingdom. Luke 4:43
It is not of this world. John 18:36
It is about peace and joy. Rom. 14:17

KINGS

Israel asked God for a king. 1 Sam. 8:5
Nations rage and kings are set against God's Anointed One. Ps. 2:1–12
God holds the king's heart. Prov. 21:1
Behold, your king is coming! Zech. 9:9
The King of kings. Rev. 17:14; 19:16

KISSES

The kisses of an enemy. Prov. 27:6
Jesus was betrayed with one. Luke 22:48
Greet with a holy kiss. Rom. 16:16

KNOWLEDGE

Tree of the knowledge of good and evil. Gen. 2:9
God's is too wonderful. Ps. 139:6
The beginning of knowledge. Prov. 1:7
Knowledge of salvation. Luke 1:77
Knowledge puffs up. 1 Cor. 8:1
Knowledge of the truth. 2 Tim. 3:7
See also Wisdom.

LAMB OF GOD

Takes away sin of the world. John 1:29, 36
A lamb without blemish. 1 Peter 1:19
Christ the Passover Lamb. 1 Cor. 5:7
Worthy is the Lamb. Rev. 5:12

LAMP

God's word is a lamp. Ps. 119:105
As a lamp, let your light shine. Matt. 5:15–16
Eye is the lamp of the body. Matt. 6:22
Seven golden lampstands. Rev. 1
See also Light.

LAW

Tablets of stone. Ex. 24:12
Obey in order to prosper. Josh. 1:8
Jesus came to fulfill the law. Matt. 5:17
Law reveals our sin. Rom. 7:7
Not a source of righteousness. Gal. 2:21
In charge until faith came. Gal. 3:24
Not made for the righteous. 1 Tim. 1:9
The royal law of love. James 2:8

LAWSUITS

Lawsuits among Christians. 1 Cor. 6:1–11

LAZINESS

Lazy hands become poor. Prov. 10:4
The slumber of the lazy. Prov. 24:30–34

The lazy, wicked servant. Matt. 25:26
See also Procrastination; Work.

LEADERSHIP

To become great, become a servant. Matt. 20:26; Mark 10:43
Christ, the head of the church. Eph. 5:23
Set an example. 1 Tim. 4:12

LEARNING

The wise hear and learn. Prov. 1:5
Learn from Jesus. Matt. 11:29
Study to show yourself approved. 2 Tim. 2:15
Continue in what you've learned. 2 Tim. 3:14
See also Discipleship; Teaching.

LEGALISM

Ignores the more important. Matt. 23:23
Legalism of the Pharisees. Luke 11:37–54
Justified apart from the law. Rom. 3:25–28
Law of liberty. Rom. 14
Not justified by works. Gal. 2:16
Human rules, traditions. Col. 2:8, 16–21

LIFE

The breath of life. Gen. 2:7
Choose life. Deut. 30:15–20
Life is not in what we own. Luke 12:15
To have abundant life. John 10:10
Jesus is the life. John 14:6
Jesus, the Word of life. 1 John 1:1
Whoever has the Son has life. 1 John 5:12
See also Eternal Life.

LIGHT

Let there be light. Gen. 1:3
God's word lights the way. Ps. 119:105
Lord will be a light. Mic. 7:8
Let your light shine. Matt. 5:16
"I am the light of the world." John 9:5
The Father of lights. James 1:17
God is light. 1 John 1:5
Walk in the light. 1 John 1:7

LISTENING *See* Hearing.

LONELINESS

Not good that man is alone. Gen. 2:18
God will never leave you. Josh. 1:5; Heb. 13:5
"For you are with me." Ps. 23:4
"I am with you always." Matt. 28:20
See also Abandonment.

LONGSUFFERING

See Patience.

LORD'S PRAYER

Our Father in heaven, hallowed be your name. Matt. 6:9–13; Luke 11:1–4

LORD'S SUPPER

See Communion.

LOST SHEEP

Sheep without a shepherd. Mark 6:34
Parable of the lost sheep. Luke 15:1–7
See also Sheep.

LOVE

Love the Lord your God. Deut. 6:5; Matt. 22:37–40; Luke 10:27
Love your neighbor. Lev. 19:18; Mark 12:31
Love covers all sins. Prov. 10:12
For God so loved the world. John 3:16
Love one another. John 13:34–35

No greater love than to lay down your life for others. John 15:13
God directed his love toward us. Rom. 5:8
Love is patient, love is kind. 1 Cor. 13
Do everything in love. 1 Cor. 16:14
This is how we know love. 1 John 3:16
God is love. 1 John 4:8
He first loved us. 1 John 4:19

LOYALTY

"Where you go I will go." Ruth 1:16
A friend loves at all times. Prov. 17:17
A friend who sticks closer than a brother. Prov. 18:24
Be found faithful. 1 Cor. 4:2
See also Faithfulness.

LUCIFER *See* Satan.

LUKEWARM

Church neither hot nor cold. Rev. 3:15–16

LUST

A covenant with one's eyes. Job 31:1
Don't lust after beauty. Prov. 6:25
Lust in the heart. Matt. 5:28
Flesh lusts against the Spirit. Gal. 5:16–17
Flee youthful lusts. 2 Tim. 2:22
Desire gives birth to sin. James 1:15
Lust of the flesh. 1 John 2:16

LYING

Shall not give false testimony. Ex. 20:16
Let lying lips be silenced. Ps. 31:18
Lying lips are an abomination. Prov. 12:22
Satan, the father of lies. John 8:44
Put away lying. Eph. 4:25
God cannot lie. Heb. 6:18
God never lies. Titus 1:2

MAGIC *See* Occult.

MANAGEMENT

See Leadership; Stewardship.

MANIPULATION

Serpent: "Did God really say?" Gen. 3:1
Priests stirred up the people. Mark 15:11
Satan disguises as angel of light. 2 Cor. 11:14

MARRIAGE

A man shall leave father and mother; become one flesh with wife. Gen. 2:24
No marriage in heaven. Matt. 22:30
Don't be unequally yoked. 2 Cor. 6:14
Honor marriage. Heb. 13:4
The wedding of the Lamb. Rev. 19:7
See also Divorce; Husbands; Wives.

MARTYRDOM

Becoming like Christ. Phil. 3:10
World not worthy of them. Heb. 11:38
Slain because of the word. Rev. 6:9

MATURITY

Once young and now old. Ps. 37:25
Put away childish things. 1 Cor. 13:11
No longer be children. Eph. 4:14
Solid food is for the mature. Heb. 5:14
See also Spiritual Growth.

MEDITATION

Meditate on God's law. Ps. 1:2; Josh. 1:8

Meditation of the heart. Ps. 19:14

Meditate on God's promises. Ps. 119:148

Think on worthy things. Phil. 4:8

MEDIATOR

Jesus, the one mediator. 1 Tim. 2:5

Mediator of new covenant. Heb. 12:24

See also INTERCESSION.

MEEKNESS

Moses was very meek. Num. 12:3

Meek crowned with victory. Ps. 149:4

Blessed are the meek. Matt. 5:5

MENTORING

Walk with the wise. Prov. 13:20

Older women to encourage younger women. Titus 2:3–5

Set an example for young men. Titus 2:6

See also DISCIPLESHIP.

MERCY

"I will have mercy on whom I have mercy." Ex. 33:19

"Mercy shall follow me." Ps. 23:6

Love mercy. Mic. 6:8

"I desire mercy, not sacrifice." Matt. 9:13

Be merciful as God is. Luke 6:36

God is rich in mercy. Eph. 2:4

Mercy in our time of need. Heb 4:16

MERCY SEAT

Place of atonement. 1 Chron. 28:11; Heb. 9:5

See also ARK OF THE COVENANT.

MESSIAH (CHRIST)

Prophecies of Messiah. Isa. 53; Jer. 23:1–7

"You are the Messiah." Matt. 16:16

The Messiah, the Christ. John 1:41

Scripture written so we might believe that Jesus is the Messiah. John 20:31

See also JESUS.

MIGHTY

How the mighty have fallen. 2 Sam. 1:19

Not by might, nor by power. Zech. 4:6

God's mighty hand lifts us up. 1 Peter 5:6

See also POWER; STRENGTH.

MILLENNIUM

Wolf and the lamb together. Isa. 65:25

Satan bound and martyrs live. Rev. 20:2–4

MIND

Love the Lord with all your mind. Matt. 22:37

Set your mind on the Spirit. Rom. 8:5–6

The renewal of your mind. Rom. 12:2

We have the mind of Christ. 1 Cor. 2:16

Have Christ's mindset. Phil. 2:5

Set mind on things above. Col. 3:2

A double minded person. James 1:8

MINISTRY

Jesus began his ministry. Luke 3:23

The ministry of the word. Acts 6:4

Ministers of the new covenant. 2 Cor. 3:6

Ministry of reconciliation. 2 Cor. 5:18

Fulfill your ministry. 2 Tim. 4:5

See also CALLING; SPIRITUAL GIFTS.

MIRACLES

Nothing is too hard for God. Jer. 32:27

Move mountains with faith. Matt. 17:20

With God all things possible. Matt. 19:26

(See next page for the miracles of Jesus.)

MIRACLES OF JESUS	MATT.	MARK	LUKE	JOHN
Healing				
Man with Leprosy	8:1–4	1:40–45	5:12–15	
Centurion's Servant	8:5–13		7:1–10	
Peter's Mother-in-law	8:14–15	1:29–31	4:38–9	
Cast out Demons	8:28–34	5:1–20	8:26–39	
Paralyzed Man	9:1–8	2:1–12	5:17–26	
Woman with Hemorrhage	9:20–22	5:25–34	8:43–48	
Two Blind Men	9:27–31			
Mute, Demon-Possessed Man	9:32–33		11:14	
Man with Shriveled Hand	12:9–13	3:1–5	6:6–10	
Blind, Mute, Possessed Man	12:22–23			
Canaanite Woman's Daughter	15:21–28	7:24–30		
Boy with a Demon	17:14–21	9:14–29	9:37–42	
Blind (Bartimaeus)	20:29–34	10:46–52	18:35–43	
Deaf Mute		7:31–37		
Possessed Man in Synagogue		1:21–28	4:31–37	
Blind Man at Bethsaida		8:22–26		
Crippled Woman			13:10–17	
Man with Dropsy			14:1–4	
Ten Lepers			17:11–19	
High Priest's Servant			22:49–51	
Official's Son				4:46–54
Sick Man at Pool of Bethesda				5:1–15
Man Born Blind				9:1–41
Power Over Nature				
Calming the Storm	8:23–27	4:35–41	8:22–25	
Feeding the 5,000	14:13–21	6:32–44	9:10–17	6:1–13
Walking on Water	14:22–33	6:45–51		6:16–21
Feeding the 4,000	15:29–38	8:1–9		
Coin in Fish	17:24–27			
Fig Tree Withered	21:18–22	11:12–14, 20–25		
Large Catch of Fish			5:4–11	
Water Turned to Wine				2:1–11
Another Large Catch of Fish				21:1–11
Raising the Dead				
Jairus's Daughter	9:18–19, 23–26	5:21–24, 35–43	8:40–42, 49–56	
Widow's Son			7:11–17	
Lazarus				11:1–44

MISSIONS

"Here I am; send me." Isa. 6:8

Those who bring good news. Isa. 52:7

Go into all the world. Mark 16:15

To the ends of the earth. Acts 1:8

How can they hear without someone preaching to them? Rom. 10:14–15

Paul became all things to all people for the sake of the gospel. 1 Cor. 9:19–23

See also EVANGELISM; WITNESSES.

MOCKERY

Wine is a mocker. Prov. 20:1

God is not to be mocked. Gal. 6:7

MONEY

God makes poor and rich. 1 Sam. 2:7

Honor God with your wealth. Prov. 3:9

A good name is better. Prov. 22:1

Lovers of it never have enough. Eccl. 5:10

Treasures in heaven. Matt. 6:19–21

Cannot serve God and money. Matt. 6:24

Gain the world, but lose soul. Mark 8:36

Love of money, root of evil. 1 Tim. 6:10

Keep your life free from the love of money. Heb. 13:5

See also STEWARDSHIP.

MONOTHEISM

None besides God. Deut. 4:35; Isa. 44:6

The Lord is one. Deut. 6:4

There is but one God. 1 Cor. 8:6

One Lord, one faith. Eph. 4:5

"I am the first and the last." Rev. 22:13

MOST HOLY PLACE

In the tabernacle. Ex. 26:33–34; Heb. 9:3

See ARK OF THE COVENANT; CURTAIN.

MOTHERS

Eve, mother of all living. Gen. 3:20

Honor father and mother. Ex. 20:12

Don't forsake mother's teaching. Prov. 1:8

Called blessed. Prov. 31:28

MOTIVES

God weighs the heart. Prov. 21:2

Motives behind spiritual actions. Matt. 6:1–18

God discerns intentions. Heb. 4:12

Wrong motives. James 4:1–3

MOUNTAINS

They melt like wax before God. Ps. 97:5

Lift eyes up to the mountains. Ps. 121:1

Mountains be shaken. Isa. 54:10

On the mountains, the feet of him who brings good news. Nah. 1:15

Move mountains with faith. Matt. 21:21

MOURNING *See* GRIEF.

MURDER

Cain rose up against Abel. Gen. 4:8

You shall not murder. Ex. 20:13

Hands that shed innocent blood. Prov. 6:16–17

Satan, murderer from beginning. John 8:44

Vengeance is the Lord's. Rom. 12:19–20

Whoever hates his brother is a murderer. 1 John 3:15

See also CAPITAL PUNISHMENT.

MUSIC

Make music to God. Ps. 149:3

Praise God with instruments. Ps. 150:1–6

Music from your heart. Eph. 5:19

See also SINGING.

NATIONS

"If my people who are called by my name . . . " 2 Chron. 7:17
God builds up and brings low. Job 12:23
God rules over nations. Ps. 22:28
Blessed is the nation whose God is the Lord. Ps. 33:12
Righteousness exalts a nation. Prov. 14:34
God will judge nations. Isa. 2:4

NATURE *See* Animals; Creation.

NEIGHBORS

Don't lie to your neighbor. Zech. 8:16
Love your neighbor as yourself. Lev. 19:18; Luke 10:27; Rom. 13:9
See also Good Samaritan.

NEW COVENANT

God will make it. Jer. 31:31; Heb. 8:8
Established on better principles. Heb. 8:6
The first is obsolete. Heb. 8:13
Jesus, the mediator of it. Heb. 12:24
See also Covenant.

NEW HEAVENS & EARTH

Former won't be remembered. Isa. 65:17
Where righteousness dwells. 2 Peter 3:13
The first will pass away. Rev. 21:1

NEW JERUSALEM

Comes down out of heaven. Rev. 3:12
The holy city. Rev. 21:2

NIGHT

God called the darkness night. Gen. 1:5
God gives songs in the night. Job 35:10
Night is coming. John 9:4
We are not of the night. 1 Thess. 5:5
As a thief in the night. 2 Peter 3:10
There will be no night there. Rev. 22:5

NOAH'S ARK

Noah, the ark, and the Flood. Gen. 6–9
Eight people saved. 1 Peter 3:20

OATHS

Don't break your word. Num. 30:2
Better not to vow, than to vow and not pay. Eccl. 5:5
Do not swear an oath. Matt. 5:34–37
Swear not by heaven or earth. James 5:12

OBEDIENCE

Blessings for obedience. Deut. 11:1–32
It is better than sacrifice. 1 Sam. 15:22
"If you love me, keep my commandments." John 14:15
Obey God rather than man. Acts 5:29

A B C D E F G H I J K L M N O P Q R S T U V W X Y Z

Jesus became obedient unto death on the cross. Phil. 2:8
Learned obedience in suffering. Heb. 5:8
This is love: to keep God's commands. 1 John 5:3

OCCULT

Don't imitate detestable ways. Deut. 18:9
Don't turn to mediums. Lev. 19:31
Astrologers burned up. Isa. 47:13–14
It will ensnare lives. Ezek. 13:18
New believers burned their books of magic arts. Acts 19:19
Practitioners go to fiery lake. Rev. 21:8

OFFERINGS

The firstfruits of all. Prov. 3:9
Thanks and freewill offerings. Amos 4:5
Through the offering of Jesus. Heb. 10:10
See also Giving; Tithes.

OLD COVENANT

See Covenant; New Covenant.

OLIVET DISCOURSE

Jesus' teaching on Mount of Olives. Matt. 24:1–25:46; Mark 13:1–37; Luke 21:5–36

OPPRESSION

Lord is a refuge for oppressed. Ps. 9:9
Human oppression. Ps. 119:134
Oppressive laws. Isa. 10:1–2
Jesus sets the oppressed free. Luke 4:18
See also Persecution.

ORDERLINESS

Set your house in order. Isa. 38:1
Do things in an orderly way. 1 Cor. 14:40
See also Confusion.

ORIGINAL SIN

The fall of mankind. Gen. 3
Entered through one man. Rom. 5:12
In Adam, all die. 1 Cor. 15:22

ORPHANS

Don't take advantage of them. Ex. 22:22
God is their helper. Ps. 10:14
A father to the fatherless. Ps. 68:5–6
Jesus won't leave us as orphans. John 14:18
Look after orphans. James 1:27

OVERCOMING

"Whom should I fear?" Ps. 27:1
Jesus has overcome the world. John 16:33
We're more than conquerors. Rom. 8:37
Overcome evil with good. Rom. 12:21
Can do all things through Christ. Phil. 4:13
We've overcome the world. 1 John 5:4

PAIN *See* Suffering.

PALM SUNDAY

Jesus' entry into Jerusalem. Matt. 21:1–11; Mark 11:1–11; Luke 9:29–44; John 12:12–19

PARABLES

"I speak to them in parables." Matt. 13:10–13; Mark 4:11; Luke 8:10
(See next page for the parables of Jesus.)

PARABLES OF JESUS	MATT.	MARK	LUKE
Lamp under a Bowl	5:14–16	4:21–22	8:16–17; 11:33–36
Wise and Foolish Builders	7:24–27		6:46–49
New Cloth on an Old Garment	9:16	2:21	5:36
New Wine in Old Wineskins	9:17	2:22	5:37–38
Sower and the Seeds	13:3–8, 18–23	4:3–8, 13–20	8:5–8, 11–15
Weeds in the Field	13:24–30, 36–43		
Mustard Seed	13:31–32	4:30–32	13:18–19
Yeast	13:33		13:20–21
Hidden Treasure	13:44		
Valuable Pearl	13:45–46		
Net of Good and Bad Fish	13:47–50		
Owner of a House	13:52		
Lost Sheep	18:12–14		15:4–7
Unmerciful Servant	18:23–35		
Workers in the Vineyard	20:1–16		
Two Sons	21:28–32		
Evil Tenants	21:33–44	12:1–11	20:9–18
Wedding Banquet	22:2–14		14:16–24
Fig Tree	24:32–35	13:28–31	21:29–33
Faithful vs. Wicked Servant	24:45–51		12:42–48
Ten Bridesmaids	25:1–13		
Talents	25:14–30		19:12–27
Sheep and Goats	25:31–46		
Growing Seed		4:26–29	
Watchful Servants		13:32–37	12:35–40
Money Lender			7:41–43
Good Samaritan			10:30–37
Friend in Need			11:5–8
Rich Fool			12:16–21
Unfruitful Fig Tree			13:6–9
Lowest Seat at the Feast			14:7–14
Cost of Discipleship			14:28–33
Lost Coin			15:8–10
Prodigal Son			15:11–32
Shrewd Manager			16:1–13
Rich Man and Lazarus			16:19–31
Master and His Servant			17:7–10
Persistent Widow			18:2–8
Pharisee and Tax Collector			18:9–14

PARADISE

"Today, you will be with me in paradise." Luke 23:43

Caught up to paradise. 2 Cor. 12:4

Where the tree of life is. Rev. 2:7

See also HEAVEN.

PARENTING

See FAMILY; FATHERS; MOTHERS.

PASSOVER

First Passover. Ex. 12

Jesus and Passover. Luke 22:7–16

Jesus the Passover Lamb. 1 Cor. 5:7

See also FEASTS; LAMB OF GOD.

PASTORS *See* ELDERS.

PATIENCE

Wait for the Lord. Ps. 37:7

Be patient in affliction. Rom. 12:12

A fruit of the Spirit. Gal. 5:22

Be patient for Lord's coming. James 5:7

God is patient. 2 Peter 3:9

PEACE

The Prince of Peace. Isa. 9:6

Wolf will dwell with the lamb. Isa. 11:6–9

Perfect peace of mind. Isa. 26:3

Blessed are the peacemakers. Matt. 5:9

Peace on earth. Luke 2:14

"My peace I give you." John 14:27

Which passes all understanding. Phil. 4:7

Lead peaceable lives. 1 Tim. 2:1–2

The Lord of peace. 2 Thess. 3:16

See also ANXIETY; WORRY.

PEARL OF GREAT PRICE

Kingdom of God is like it. Matt. 13:45–46

PENTECOST

Holy Spirit came upon believers. Acts 2

See also TONGUES.

PERFECT

God's works are perfect. Deut. 32:4

God's law is perfect. Ps. 19:7

Be perfect as God is perfect. Matt. 5:48

Made perfect by suffering. Heb. 5:8–9

Law made nothing perfect. Heb. 7:19

Every perfect gift is from above. James 1:17

Perfect love casts out fear. 1 John 4:18

PERSECUTION

Persecuted but still following. Ps. 119:157

Blessed are the persecuted. Matt. 5:10–11

Pray for persecutors. Matt. 5:44

Bless persecutors. Rom. 12:14

Persecuted but not forsaken. 2 Cor. 4:9

Expect persecution. 2 Tim. 3:12

For righteousness' sake. 1 Peter 3:14

Insulted because of Christ. 1 Peter 4:14

See also OPPRESSION; SUFFERING.

PERSEVERANCE

Persist in doing good. Rom. 2:7

Love endures all things. 1 Cor. 13:7

Do not tire of doing good; we'll reap in due season. Gal. 6:9

Keep on praying. Eph. 6:18

"I have finished the race." 2 Tim. 4:7

Run with perseverance. Heb. 12:1

Testing produces perseverance. James 1:3

See also ENDURANCE; RACE.

PHARISEES

Generation of vipers. Matt. 3:7

Want the best seats. Luke 11:43

Confident of own righteousness. Luke 18:9
Love the praise of others. John 12:43
See also Hypocrisy; Legalism.

PHILOSOPHY

Empty philosophy. Col. 2:8
See also Reason; Wisdom.

PHYSICIAN

A king who sought doctors, not God. 2 Chron. 16:12
Physician, heal yourself! Luke 4:23
Healthy don't need a doctor. Luke 5:31

PLAGUES

Plagues upon Egypt. Ex. 7–11
The bowls of wrath. Rev. 15–16

PLANNING

Commit plans to the Lord. Prov. 16:3
The plans of the diligent. Prov. 21:5
Many plans are in a heart. Prov. 19:21
"For I know the plans I have for you." Jer. 29:11
First consider the cost. Luke 14:28
Say, "If the Lord wills." James 4:15

PLEASING OTHERS

Please neighbors for their good. Rom. 15:2
Trying to please people is not being God's servant. Gal. 1:10

POOR

God is maker of rich and poor. Prov. 22:2
Better to be poor and blameless. Prov. 28:6
Neither poverty nor riches. Prov. 30:8
Defend their rights. Prov. 31:8–9
The poor in spirit. Matt. 5:3
Rich man and Lazarus. Luke 16:19–31
Jesus became poor. 2 Cor. 8:9
See also Giving; Wealth.

PORNOGRAPHY

See Lust; Sexual Immorality.

POSSESSIONS

Hoarding from others. Prov. 11:26
Your heart is wherever your treasure is. Matt. 6:21
Sell your possessions. Matt. 19:21
Life is not about possessions. Luke 12:14
Believers shared possessions. Acts 2:45
Possessions without love. 1 John 3:17–18

POWER

God is excellent in power. Job 37:23
One wise person is better than ten powerful rulers. Eccl. 7:19
God gives power to the faint. Isa. 40:29
We wrestle against principalities and powers. Eph. 6:12
Delivered from darkness' power. Col. 1:13
The word of God is powerful. Heb. 4:12
See also Mighty; Strength.

PRAISE

God is worthy of praise. 2 Sam. 22:4
God is greatly praised. 1 Chron. 16:25
Earth is full of God's praise. Hab. 3:3
Offer the sacrifice of praise. Heb. 13:15
See also Adoration; Worship.

PRAYER

"Before they call I will answer." Isa. 65:24
Call to God, he will answer you. Jer. 33:3
The Lord's Prayer. Matt. 6:9–13; Luke 11:1–4
Ask and receive. Matt. 7:7; Mark 11:24
Where two or three gather. Matt. 18:20

Be faithful in prayer. Rom. 12:12
Pray in the Spirit. Eph. 6:18
Pray without ceasing. 1 Thess. 5:17
Powerful prayers of righteous. James 5:16
God hears our prayers. 1 Peter 3:12

PREACHING

Jesus preached the kingdom. Matt. 4:23
Preach Christ crucified. 1 Cor. 1:23
Compelled to preach. 1 Cor. 9:6
Appointed to preach. 2 Tim. 1:11
In season and out of season. 2 Tim. 4:2
See also EVANGELISM; MISSIONS.

PREDESTINATION

See ELECTION.

PRESENCE OF GOD

God will go with you. Ex. 33:14
"Where can I go from your presence?" Ps. 139:7
Jesus is where we gather. Matt. 18:20
"I am with you always." Matt. 28:20
Jesus in God's presence. Heb. 9:24

PRESERVATION OF GOD'S WORD

It is settled in heaven. Ps. 119:89
It will stand forever. Isa. 40:8
Not one jot or tittle will pass. Matt. 5:18
It will never pass away. Matt. 24:35
Add anything, suffer plagues. Rev. 22:18
Delete anything, lose life. Rev. 22:19

PRIDE

God hates a proud look. Prov. 6:17
Pride goes before a fall. Prov. 16:18
Do nothing from vain conceit. Phil. 2:3
God opposes the proud. James 4:6; 1 Peter 5:5
Pride of life is not of God. 1 John 2:16
See also ARROGANCE; BOASTING.

PRIESTHOOD/PRIESTS

The priest Melchizedek. Gen. 14:18; Heb. 7
Jesus is the one Mediator. 1 Tim. 2:5
Jesus is our High Priest. Heb. 3:1
We are a royal priesthood. 1 Peter 2:9
We are priests. Rev. 1:6

PRIORITIES

Have no other gods. Ex. 20:3
Seek first God's kingdom. Matt. 6:33

PRISONERS

Proclaim liberty to the captives. Isa. 61:1; Luke 4:18
Visit those in prison. Matt. 25:36
Prisoner of the law of sin. Rom. 7:23
Prisoner of Christ. Eph. 3:1
Remember those in prison. Heb. 13:3

PROCRASTINATION

Don't delay to obey God. Ps. 119:60
Don't be a sluggard. Prov. 6:9
Make the best use of time. Eph. 5:16

PRODIGAL SON

Parable of the lost son. Luke 15:11–32
See also BACKSLIDING.

PROMISED LAND

Promise to Abraham. Gen. 12
Land of milk and honey. Josh. 5:6
Lord gave Israel the land. Josh. 21:43

PROMISES OF GOD

Not one failed. Josh. 21:45
Promise of peace to his people. Ps. 85:8

God is trustworthy. Ps. 145:13
All are "yes" in Christ. 2 Cor. 1:20
We have these promises. 2 Cor. 7:1
Promise of life in Jesus. 2 Tim. 1:1
Great and precious promises. 2 Peter 1:4
God is not slow concerning his promises. 2 Peter 3:9

PROPHECY/PROPHETS

Reveals secrets to prophets. Amos 3:7
Sons, daughters will prophesy. Acts 2:17
From Holy Spirit, not man. 2 Peter 1:21
False prophets. 2 Peter 2:1
Many false prophets. 1 John 4:1

PROSPERITY *See* Success.

PROTECTION

God is our rock. 2 Sam. 22:2
Our fortress. Ps. 18:2
Our stronghold. Ps. 27:1
Shelter of the Most High. Ps. 91:1
God is with us. Isa. 41:10
Stronghold in day of trouble. Nah. 1:7
Lord promises no harm. Acts 18:10
Protection from evil one. 2 Thess. 3:3
See also Presence of God; Refuge.

PROVISION

God supplied everything. Ps. 104
Cares about everything. Matt. 10:29
Provides for our needs. Acts 14:17
Can do more than we ask. Eph. 3:20
Will supply all your needs. Phil. 4:19

PUNISHMENT

Generational punishment. Ex. 34:6–7
Wicked won't go unpunished. Prov. 11:21
Everlasting punishment. Matt. 25:46
Wrongs will be repaid. Col. 3:25
Vengeance belongs to God. Heb. 10:30
See also Discipline; Revenge.

PURITY

"Create in me a pure heart." Ps. 51:10
Path of purity. Ps. 119:9
Blessed are the pure in heart. Matt. 5:8
Washed through God's word. Eph. 5:27
Think on whatever is pure. Phil. 4:8
Keep yourself pure. 1 Tim. 5:22
Purify our hearts. James 4:8
See also Clean.

PURPOSE

Everything for its purpose. Prov. 16:4
A time to every purpose. Eccl. 3:1
God's purpose will stand. Isa. 46:10
All things work together for good for those called to God's purpose. Rom. 8:28
The eternal purpose. Eph. 3:11
See also Duty.

QUARRELING

A quarreling spouse. Prov. 25:24
Forgive grievances. Col. 3:13
Avoid foolish controversies. Titus 3:9
Caused by selfish desires. James 4:1
See also Conflict.

QUIETNESS

Restrain your words. Prov. 17:27
A time to be silent. Eccl. 3:7
Better than useless desires. Eccl. 4:6
Strength is in quietness. Isa. 30:15
God will quiet you by his love. Zeph. 3:17
Lead a quiet life. 1 Thess. 4:11
Learn in quietness. 1 Tim. 2:11
Gentle and quiet spirit. 1 Peter 3:4

RACE, SPIRITUAL

Race for the prize. 1 Cor. 9:24–27
Have not run in vain. Phil. 2:16
Have finished the race. 2 Tim. 4:7–8
Run with perseverance. Heb. 12:1–2

RAIN

Forty days and forty nights. Gen. 7:4
God's word is like rain. Isa. 55:10–11
God sends rain on everyone. Matt. 5:45
God is kind by giving rain. Acts 14:17

RAINBOW

A sign of the covenant. Gen. 9:16
Rainbow around the throne. Rev. 4:3

RAPTURE, THE

Caught up together in the clouds. 1 Thess. 4:16–17

REASON

Come now, let us reason. Isa. 1:18
Once reasoned like a child. 1 Cor. 13:11
Be ready to give a reason. 1 Peter 3:15
See also PHILOSOPHY; WISDOM.

REBELLION

Like the sin of divination. 1 Sam. 15:23
An evil man seeks rebellion. Prov. 17:11
Children against parents. Mark 13:12
Against authorities. Rom. 13:2
The rebellion and man of lawlessness. 2 Thess. 2:3
See also DISOBEDIENCE.

REBUKE

Open rebuke is better than hidden love. Prov. 27:5
God will no longer rebuke. Zeph. 3:17
Jesus rebuked demons. Matt. 17:18
Rebuke and forgive. Luke 17:3
Rebuke those who persist in sin. 1 Tim. 5:20
See also DISCIPLINE.

REDEMPTION

"I know my redeemer lives!" Job 19:25
Redemption is precious. Ps. 49:8
With God, full redemption. Ps. 130:7
Redemption draws near. Luke 2:38
Redemption of our bodies. Rom. 8:23
Sealed until day of redemption. Eph. 4:30
Through Jesus' blood. Col. 1:14
Jesus obtained eternal redemption for us. Heb. 9:12

REFUGE

Refuge in God's wings. Ruth 2:12 ; Ps. 91:4

God is our refuge. Ps. 46:1; 62:8; 142:5
Strength, fortress, refuge. Jer. 16:19
A refuge in times of trouble. Nah. 1:7
See also PROTECTION; ROCKS.

REGENERATION

The regeneration of all things. Matt. 19:28
By the washing of regeneration. Titus 3:5

REGRET

Remember not former things. Isa. 43:18
Godly sorrow. 2 Cor. 7:10
Forget the past. Phil. 3:13

REJECTION

They rejected God. 1 Sam 8:7
Cornerstone rejected. Ps. 118:22; Matt. 21:42
Jesus rejected by people. Isa. 53:3
Reject Jesus, reject the Father. Luke 10:16
Rejection of Jesus means death. John 3:36
Reject teaching, reject God. 1 Thess. 4:8
See also HATRED; PERSECUTION.

REJOICE

Rejoice and be glad! Ps. 118:24
Don't rejoice over enemies. Prov. 24:17
Rejoice in salvation. Luke 10:20
Rejoice in suffering. Rom. 5:3
Rejoice with those who do. Rom. 12:15
Rejoice in the truth. 1 Cor. 13:6
Rejoice in the Lord always. Phil 4:4
See also JOY; PRAISE.

RELATIONSHIPS

See FAMILY; FRIENDS; NEIGHBORS.

RELIGION

Put religion into practice. 1 Tim. 5:4
Religion accepted by God. James 1:26–27

REPENTANCE

"If my people, who are called by my name . . . " 2 Chron. 7:14
Jesus preached, "Repent!" Matt. 4:17
Jesus came to call sinners. Luke 5:32
Repent so that times of refreshing will come. Acts 3:19
Brought by godly sorrow. 2 Cor. 7:10
God wants all to repent. 2 Peter 3:9

REPUTATION

Known by one's actions. Prov. 20:11
Good name better than riches. Prov. 22:1
Avoid every form of evil. 1 Thess. 5:22
Keep conduct honorable. 1 Peter 2:12
See also CHARACTER.

RESPECT

Show respect for elders. Lev. 19:32
Wives, respect husbands. Eph. 5:33
Respect those who labor. 1 Thess. 5:12
Proper respect to everyone. 1 Peter 2:17
Husbands, respect wives. 1 Peter 3:7
See also FEAR OF THE LORD.

RESPONSIBILITY

The good and right way. 1 Sam. 12:23–24
Carry your own load. Gal. 6:5
Use what God has given you. 1 Tim. 4:14
See also STEWARDSHIP.

REST

God rested on the seventh day. Gen. 2:2
"I will give you rest." Ex. 33:14
Lie down in green pastures. Ps. 23:2
Jesus gives rest. Matt. 11:28
Enter God's rest. Heb. 4:1–11
See also SABBATH.

RESTORATION

Job restored after suffering. Job 42:10
"Restore to me the joy of your salvation." Ps. 51:12
Years restored. Joel 2:25
Jesus restored Peter. John 21:15–25
Restore sinners. Gal. 6:1
God will restore you. 1 Peter 5:10
The restoration of all things. Rev. 21

RESURRECTION

Not abandoned to the grave. Ps. 16:10
Messiah raised on third day. Luke 24:46
"I am the resurrection." John 11:25
Death can't keep its hold. Acts 2:24–28
Buried and raised with Christ. Rom. 6:4
Spirit will raise believers. Rom. 8:11
Christ died, buried, raised. 1 Cor. 15:3–4
The dead raised imperishable in the twinkling of an eye. 1 Cor. 15:52

RETURN OF CHRIST

See SECOND COMING.

REVELATION

God reveals mysteries. Job. 12:22
Lack of it leads to sin. Prov. 29:18
Glory of God revealed. Isa. 40:5
Mystery made known. Eph. 3:3; Col. 1:26
It is from Jesus Christ. Rev. 1:1

REVENGE

God revenges. Nah. 1:2
Turn the other cheek. Matt. 5:39
Vengeance is the Lord's. Rom. 12:19
Don't repay evil for evil. 1 Thess. 5:15
Jesus didn't retaliate. 1 Peter 2:23
See also JUSTICE.

REWARDS

God gives desires of your heart. Ps. 37:4
Treasures in heaven. Matt. 6:19
Repaid according to actions. Matt. 16:27
Rewards are great. Luke 6:23
An inheritance from God. Col. 3:23–24
Rewarded with crown of life. James 1:12

RICH

Rich young ruler. Matt. 9:16–30; Mark 10:17–31; Luke 18:18–30
Rich man and Lazarus. Luke 16:19–31
Be rich toward God. Luke 12:21
Rich in generosity. 2 Cor. 8:2
Rich in good works. 1 Tim. 6:18
See also POSSESSIONS; WEALTH.

RIGHTEOUSNESS

The righteous live by faith. Hab. 2:4
God leads in righteous paths. Ps. 23:3
Walk in way of righteousness. Prov. 8:20
God is our righteousness. Jer. 23:6
Those who thirst for it. Matt. 5:6
We become righteousness. 2 Cor. 5:21
Breastplate of righteousness. Eph. 6:14
A crown of righteousness. 2 Tim. 4:8

ROCKS

The Rock their Savior. Deut. 32:15
"The Lord is my rock." Ps. 18:2
Set high upon a rock. Ps. 27:5
Build a foundation on rock. Luke 6:48
The rocks will cry out. Luke 19:40
Christ our Rock. 1 Cor. 10:4
See also CORNERSTONE; PROTECTION.

RULERS

See AUTHORITY; GOVERNMENT.

SABBATH

God rested on the seventh day. Gen 2:3
Remember the Sabbath day. Ex. 20:8
It was made for man. Mark 2:27
Son of Man is Lord of it. Luke 6:5
See also Rest.

SACRED *See* Holiness.

SACRIFICE

God desires mercy over sacrifice. Hos. 6:6
Your bodies a living sacrifice. Rom. 12:1
The one sacrifice for sins. Heb. 10:12
Sacrifice of praise. Heb. 13:15

SAFETY

Lie down in safety. Ps. 4:8
God will not let your foot slip. Ps. 121:3
Safety in many counselors. Prov. 11:14
Dwell in secure homes. Isa. 32:18
See also Protection; Refuge.

SALT

The salt of the earth. Matt. 5:13
Season speech with salt. Col. 4:6

SALVATION

The joy of your salvation. Ps. 51:12
All will see salvation of God. Isa. 52:10
Whoever believes in Jesus. John 3:16
The Father draws them near. John 6:44
Salvation in no other name. Acts 4:12
Gospel brings salvation Rom. 1:16
Christ died for us. Rom. 5:8
Confess and believe. Rom. 10:9
It's nearer than we believed. Rom. 13:11
Saved through faith. Eph. 2:8–9
Helmet of salvation. Eph. 6:17
Salvation was confirmed. Heb. 2:3
Jesus is the source. Heb. 2:9
See also Born Again; Eternal Life.

SANCTIFICATION

God sanctifies. Ezek. 20:12
Sanctified by truth. John 17:17–19
Sanctification is God's will. 1 Thess. 4:3
Through Jesus' blood. Heb. 13:12
Work of the Spirit. 1 Peter 1:2

SANCTUARY

Praise God in his sanctuary. Ps. 150:1
A shadow of what's in heaven. Heb. 8:5
See also Tabernacle; Temple.

SATAN

Ancient serpent. Gen. 3:1; Rev. 12:9; 20:2
Satan roams the earth. Job 1:7
Lucifer. Isa. 14:12
Beelzebub. Matt. 12:24
"Get behind me, Satan!" Matt. 16:23
He takes away the word. Mark 4:15
He fell from heaven. Luke 10:18
He is the father of lies. John 8:44
God will crush Satan. Rom. 16:20
Don't give the devil a foothold. Eph. 4:27
He poses as an angel of light. 2 Cor. 11:14
He prowls like a lion. 1 Peter 5:8
Satan will flee from you. James 4:7

SAVIOR *See* JESUS; MESSIAH.

SCRIPTURE

Scripture of truth. Dan. 10:21
Scripture is fulfilled. Luke 4:21
Scripture must be fulfilled. Acts 1:16
God-breathed and useful. 2 Tim. 3:16
See also WORD OF GOD.

SECOND COMING

Christ coming with clouds. Dan. 7:13
Christ will come in glory. Matt. 25:31
Will return like he ascended. Acts 1:11
Will appear a second time. Heb. 9:28
See also END TIMES; RAPTURE.

SEEDS

The seed is God's word. Luke 8:11
Faith like a mustard seed. Luke 17:6
Dead kernel, many seeds. John 12:24
God makes it grow. 1 Cor. 3:6
Abraham's seed, Christ. Gal. 3:16
Imperishable seed. 1 Peter 1:23
See also HARVEST; SOWING.

SEEKING

Seek God and you'll find him. Deut. 4:29
Seek while God may be found. Isa. 55:6
Seek God with all your heart. Jer. 29:13
Seek first God's kingdom. Matt. 6:33
Seek and you will find. Luke 11:9-10

SELF-CONTROL

Like a city with broken walls. Prov. 25:28
Every athlete trains. 1 Cor. 9:25–27
A fruit of the Spirit. Gal. 5:22–23
Teach older men to have it. Titus 2:2
Urge younger men to have it. Titus 2:6
Have it for your prayers' sake. 1 Peter 4:7

SELFISHNESS

Not for selfish gain. Ps. 119:36
Seek the interest of neighbor. 1 Cor. 10:24
Love is not self-seeking. 1 Cor. 13:5
Look to the interest of others. Phil. 2:3–4
People will be lovers of selves. 2 Tim. 3:2

SELF-RIGHTEOUSNESS

Tax collector and Pharisee. Luke 18:9–14
Saved by mercy, not deeds. Titus 3:5
It deceives oneself. James 1:26
See also ARROGANCE; HYPOCRISY.

SERMON ON THE MOUNT

Jesus' teachings. Matt. 5–7

SERPENT

Serpent's head will be crushed. Gen. 3:15
Son of Man lifted up as Moses lifted the snake in the wilderness. John 3:14
Satan the ancient serpent. Rev. 12:9; 20:2

SERVANTS

Formed to be God's servant. Isa. 49:5
Good and faithful servant. Matt. 25:21
Jesus, the example of servant. John 13:15
No longer a servant, but a son. Gal. 4:7
Jesus became like a servant. Phil. 2:7
Subject to their masters. Titus 2:9

SEX

Be fruitful and multiply. Gen. 1:28
"My lover is mine, I am his." Song 2:16
Become one flesh. Mark 10:8
Do not deprive your spouse. 1 Cor. 7:1–8
Keep the marriage bed pure. Heb. 13:4

SEXUAL IMMORALITY

The body is not for it. 1 Cor. 6:13

Flee from it. 1 Cor. 6:18
Not a hint of it. Eph. 5:3
Learn self-control. 1 Thess. 4:3–5
See also Adultery; Lust.

SHAME

Hope in God, never be shamed. Ps. 25:3
Instead of shame, a double portion of inheritance. Isa. 61:7
Do not be ashamed of Jesus. Luke 9:26
Not ashamed of the gospel. Rom. 1:16–17
Believe in Jesus and never be shamed. Rom. 9:33; 10:11
Foolish things shame the wise. 1 Cor. 1:27
Jesus ignored the shame. Heb. 12:2
Not ashamed of testimony. 2 Tim. 1:8
Not ashamed of suffering. 1 Peter 4:16

SHEEP

We like sheep have gone astray. Isa. 53:6
Parable of sheep and goats. Matt. 25:31–46
"Feed my sheep." John 21:17
Like sheep to the slaughter. Rom. 8:36
Sheep gone astray. 1 Peter 2:25
See also Lamb of God; Lost Sheep.

SHEPHERD

"The Lord is my shepherd." Ps. 23:1
Strike shepherd, sheep scatter. Matt. 26:31
Jesus, the good Shepherd. John 10:14
Jesus, the great Shepherd. Heb. 13:20
Chief Shepherd will appear. 1 Peter 5:4

SICKNESS *See* Illness.

SIGHT

Nothing wicked before my eyes. Ps. 101:3
The pure in heart will see God. Matt. 5:8
"I was blind, but now I see!" John 9:25
Now we see through a glass darkly, but will see face to face. 1 Cor 13:12
Walk by faith, not by sight. 2 Cor. 5:7
See also Blindness; Eyes.

SIN

Sin lies at the door. Gen. 4:7
Your sin will find you out. Num. 32:23
All have sinned. Rom. 3:23
The wages of sin is death. Rom. 6:23
Whatever is not of faith. Rom. 14:23
It is the sting of death. 1 Cor. 15:56
Failure to do right thing. James 4:17
Saying we have no sin. 1 John 1:8
Sin is lawlessness. 1 John 3:4
See also Forgiveness; Original Sin.

SINCERITY

Love must be sincere. Rom. 12:9
Godly sincerity. 2 Cor. 1:12
Sincere faith. 1 Tim. 1:5
Sincere love. 1 Peter 1:22

SINGING

Shout joyfully to God. Ps. 66:1
Enter God's presence singing. Ps. 100
God sings over us. Zeph. 3:17
Sing with grace in your heart. Col. 3:16
Sing when happy. James 5:13
They sang a new song. Rev. 5:9

SINGLENESS

Good to remain single. 1 Cor. 7:7–9, 32–38

SLAVES

Proclaim liberty to the captive. Luke 4:18
No longer slave to sin. Rom. 6:6
Slaves to righteousness. Rom. 6:15–23
Neither slave nor free in Christ. Gal. 3:28

The yoke of slavery. Gal. 5:1
Slaves obey masters. Eph. 6:5
Treat slaves justly. Col. 4:1
Not a slave, but a brother. Philem. 1:16

SOLDIERS

Put on the armor of God. Eph. 6:11
Good soldier of Christ. 2 Tim. 2:3–4

SON OF GOD

Son of the Living God. Matt. 16:16
Truly, the Son of God! Matt. 27:54
God sent his only Son. John 3:16
Son of God has come. 1 John 5:20

SONGS *See* SINGING.

SONS *See* CHILDREN.

SORROW

Sorrow is better than laughter. Eccl. 7:3
Godly sorrow brings repentance. 2 Cor. 7:10
Sorrow upon sorrow. Phil. 2:27
See also GRIEF; SUFFERING.

SOUL

Breath of life from God. Gen. 2:7
All people belong to God. Ezek. 18:4
"He restores my soul." Ps. 23:3
Fear him who can destroy it. Matt. 10:28
Gain the world, forfeit soul. Matt. 16:26
Love God with all your soul. Mark 12:30
My soul magnifies God. Luke 1:46
Dividing soul and spirit. Heb. 4:12

SOVEREIGNTY

God above all. 1 Chron. 29:11–12
Lord gives and Lord takes away. Job 1:21
The Lord does what he pleases. Ps. 135:6

SOWING

Sow in tears, reap in joy. Ps. 126:5
Sown much, brought in little. Hag. 1:6
Parable of the sower. Luke 8:4–15
Will reap what you sow. Gal. 6:7
Sow sparingly, reap sparingly. 2 Cor. 9:6
See also HARVEST; SEEDS.

SPEECH

Guard your lips. Ps. 141:3
Death and life in our words. Prov. 18:21
The mouth speaks what is in the heart. Matt. 12:34–37
Your speech betrays you. Matt. 26:73
Speak truth in love. Eph. 4:15
No unwholesome talk. Eph. 4:29
Rid yourself of filthy language. Col. 3:8
Speech should be full of grace. Col. 4:6
Be slow to speak. James 1:19
See also TONGUE.

SPIRIT *See* HOLY SPIRIT; SOUL.

SPIRITUAL DISCIPLINES

Meditate on God's words. Josh. 1:8
Prayer and fasting. Mark 9:29
Search the Scriptures daily. Acts 17:11
Train yourself for godliness. 1 Tim. 4:7
Be able to teach others. 2 Tim. 2:2
Correctly handle God's Word. 2 Tim. 2:15

SPIRITUAL GIFTS

Different gifts. Rom. 12:6–8; 1 Cor. 12:4–30
Desire spiritual gifts. 1 Cor. 14:1
To equip believers. Eph. 4:11–12

SPIRITUAL GROWTH

So not to sin against God. Ps. 119:11
Infants in Christ. 1 Cor. 3:1–2

Put childish ways behind you. 1 Cor. 13:11
Mature and fully assured. Col. 4:12
Let us go on to maturity. Heb. 6:1
Grow up in salvation. 1 Peter 2:2

SPIRITUAL WARFARE

The whole armor of God. Eph. 6:11
We wrestle not against flesh and blood. Eph. 6:12
War in heaven. Rev. 12:7
See also ARMOR OF GOD.

STARS

A star out of Jacob. Num. 24:17
God set stars in their place. Ps. 8:3–4
God names the stars. Ps. 147:4
Stars will fall from heaven. Isa. 13:10; Mark 13:25
Star of Bethlehem. Matt. 2:2
Morning star rises in hearts. 2 Peter 1:19

STEALING

"You shall not steal." Ex. 20:15
Stop stealing. Eph. 4:28
See also CHEATING; THIEVES.

STEWARDSHIP

Dominion over the earth. Gen. 1:28
To whom much is given, much is required. Luke 12:48
Trusted with little and much. Luke 16:10
Faithful stewards of grace. 1 Peter 4:10
See also MONEY; RESPONSIBILITY.

STORMS

God spoke from the whirlwind. Job. 38:1
God calms the storm. Ps. 107:29
God's way is in the storm. Nah. 1:3
Jesus calmed a storm. Mark 4:39

STRENGTH

"The Lord is my strength." Ex. 15:2
Joy of the Lord is your strength. Neh. 8:10
Strength for the weary. Isa. 40:29–31
God is our strength. Hab. 3:19
Strength in weakness. 2 Cor. 12:9
"I can do all things through Christ who strengthens me." Phil. 4:13
See also MIGHTY; POWER.

STRESS

Don't be discouraged. Isa. 41:10
Don't worry about tomorrow. Matt. 6:34
Don't be troubled. John 14:27
Cast all your cares on God. 1 Peter 5:7
See also ANXIETY; WORRY.

STRUGGLES

God will fight for you. Ex. 14:14
God's plan of hope. Jer. 29:11
Troubles won't last long. 2 Cor. 4:17
God's grace is sufficient. 2 Cor. 12:9
See also OVERCOMING.

SUBMISSION

Trust God completely. Prov. 3:5
Submit to one another. Eph. 5:21–22
Submit to God. James 4:7
Younger submit to older. 1 Peter 5:5
Submit to rulers. Titus 3:1
See also AUTHORITY.

SUCCESS

Follow God's rules. Josh. 1:8
Delight in God and prosper. Ps. 1:1–3
Gain the world, but lose soul. Matt. 16:26
Lose everything, gain Christ. Phil. 3:7–8
See also PLANNING.

SUFFERING

Christ, a Man of suffering. Isa. 53:3–4
It produces perseverance. Rom. 5:3–5
Present suffering is nothing compared to coming glory. Rom. 8:18
Rejoice in suffering. Col. 1:24
Prophets are an example. James 5:10
Suffering for what is right. 1 Peter 3:14
No more suffering. Rev. 21:4
See also SORROW; TRIALS.

SUICIDE

God heals the brokenhearted. Ps. 147:3
Why die before your time? Eccl. 7:17
Nothing can separate us from God's love. Rom. 8:39

SUN

The sun stood still. Josh. 10:13
No new thing under the sun. Eccl. 1:9
Sun will turn into darkness. Acts 2:20
God's glory is the city's light. Rev. 21:23

SWORDS

Make swords into plowshares. Isa. 2:4
Not peace, but a sword. Matt. 10:34
Use the sword, die by sword. Matt. 26:52
Sell cloak, buy sword. Luke 22:36
Sword of the Spirit. Eph. 6:17
God's word sharper than sword. Heb. 4:12

SYMPATHY

Weep with those who weep. Rom. 12:15
If one believer suffers, all do. 1 Cor. 12:26
Comfort others in trouble. 2 Cor. 1:3–4
Carry each others' burdens. Gal. 6:2
Jesus sympathizes with us. Heb. 4:16
Be sympathetic. 1 Peter 3:8

TABERNACLE

God designed the tabernacle. Ex. 25:9
A greater, more perfect one. Heb. 9:11
See also SANCTUARY.

TALK *See* SPEECH.

TASTE

The wicked enjoy the taste of evil. Job 20:12–14
Taste and see, the Lord is good. Ps. 34:8
God's words are sweetest. Ps. 119:103

TAXES

Kings of earth collect taxes. Matt. 17:25
Give to Caesar what is Caesar's. Matt. 22:21; Luke 20:25
Pay what is owed. Rom. 13:6-7

TEACHERS/TEACHING

Diligently teach God's words to children. Deut. 6:4–9
Jesus taught with authority. Matt. 7:29
Holy Spirit will teach you. John 14:26
Teach and preach always. Acts 5:42
Spiritual gift. Rom. 12:7; 1 Cor. 12:28; Eph. 4:11
Scripture is profitable for it. 2 Tim. 3:16–17
Need someone to teach. Heb. 5:12
Teachers judged more strictly. James 3:1
See also FALSE TEACHERS; LEARNING.

TEARS

"List my tears on your scroll." Ps. 56:8
Sow in tears, reap in joy. Ps. 126:5
Jesus' feet washed with tears. Luke 7:38
There will be no more tears. Rev. 21:4
See also GRIEF; WEEPING.

TEMPLE

Solomon built first temple. 1 Kings 9:1
Jesus found in the temple. Luke 2:46
If destroyed, Jesus will raise it. John 2:19
Your body, Holy Spirit's temple. 1 Cor. 6:19
God's temple in heaven. Rev. 11:19

TEMPTATION

Jesus in the wilderness. Mark 1:13
Lead us not into temptation. Luke 11:4
A way to escape it. 1 Cor. 10:13
Jesus, tempted like us. Heb. 2:18; 4:15
God cannot be tempted. James 1:13

TEN COMMANDMENTS

God's commands. Ex. 20:1–17; Deut. 5:1–22

TESTIMONY

Shall not give false testimony. Ex. 20:16.
False witness tells lies. Prov. 12:17
Jesus didn't need man's. John 2:25
God's testimony is greater. 1 John 5:9
See also WITNESSES.

TESTING OF FAITH

Abraham tested by God. Gen. 22:1–19
Testing produces patience. James 1:2–3
Sufferings prove faith. 1 Peter 1:7
See also TRIALS.

THANKFULNESS

Come before God with thanks. Ps. 95:2
Enter gates with thanksgiving. Ps. 100:4
Give thanks to God; he is good. Ps. 107:1
Thank God for his gifts. 2 Cor. 9:15
Give thanks for all things. Eph. 5:20
Pray with thanksgiving. Phil. 4:6
In everything, give thanks. 1 Thess. 5:18

THIEVES

Lord hates robbery. Isa. 61:8
No thief can steal your treasures in heaven. Luke 12:33
Comes to steal, kill, destroy. John 10:10
Day of the Lord will come like a thief in the night. 1 Thess. 5:2; 2 Peter 3:10
See also STEALING.

THIRST

Give water to thirsty enemy. Prov. 25:21
"I was thirsty and you gave me something." Matt. 25:35
"Whoever believes in me will never thirst." John 6:35
Jesus thirsted on the cross. John 19:28

THORN IN THE FLESH

Paul's thorn in the flesh. 2 Cor. 12:7–10

THOUGHTS

God knows your thoughts. Ps. 94:11
God's thoughts are not ours. Isa. 55:8
Evil thoughts from the heart. Matt. 15:19
Take every thought captive. 2 Cor. 10:5
Think on excellent things. Phil. 4:8
God judges our thoughts. Heb. 4:12

THRONE OF GOD

It will last forever. Heb. 1:8
Jesus at the right hand of it. Heb. 12:2
God's throne in heaven. Rev. 7:15

TIME/TIMING

It is in God's hand. Ps. 31:15
There's a time for everything. Eccl. 3:1–8
All is beautiful in its time. Eccl. 3:11
Not good to know times, dates. Acts 1:7
When the time had fully come. Gal. 4:4
Make the most of time. Eph. 5:16
Christ the same yesterday, today, and forever. Heb. 13:8
A thousand years like one day. 2 Peter 3:8

TIRED *See* WEARINESS.

TITHES

A portion of all is God's. Lev. 27:30
Bring the whole tithe to God. Mal. 3:10
Hypocrisy in tithing. Matt. 23:23
See also GIVING; OFFERINGS.

TONGUE

Guard your tongue. Prov. 21:23
Every tongue to confess God. Rom. 14:11
Every tongue confess Jesus. Phil. 2:11
Taming the tongue. James 3:1–12
Keep your tongue from evil. 1 Peter 3:10
See also SPEECH.

TONGUES, SPEAKING IN

Tongues of fire at Pentecost. Acts 2:1–13
Spiritual gift of tongues. 1 Cor. 12:10; 14
Tongues of angels. 1 Cor. 13:1

TOWER OF BABEL

An ungodly tower. Gen. 11:1–9

TRANSFORMATION

The renewing your mind. Rom 12:2
We will all be changed. 1 Cor. 15:51
Transformed into God's image. 2 Cor. 3:18
A new creation in Christ. 2 Cor. 5:17
To be like Jesus' body. Phil. 3:21
See also SPIRITUAL GROWTH.

TREASURES

God's treasured possession. Mal. 3:17
Treasures in heaven. Matt. 6:19–21; 19:21
Hidden treasure. Matt. 13:44–46
Where your heart is. Luke 12:34
Treasure in jars of clay. 2 Cor. 4:7

TREES

Trees in the Garden of Eden. Gen. 2:16
Planted by rivers of water. Ps. 1:3
Tree is known by its fruit. Luke 6:44
Cursed to hang on a tree. Gal. 3:13
Tree of life in heaven. Rev. 22:2

TRIALS

God is with you through trials. Isa. 43:2
In the midst of a severe trial. 2 Cor. 8:2
Some faced jeers, flogging. Heb. 11:36
Consider trials pure joy. James 1:2
To test your faith. 1 Peter 1:7; 4:12
See also SUFFERING; TESTING OF FAITH.

TRIBULATION

It will be great. Matt. 24:21
Those who came out of it. Rev. 7:14
See also END TIMES; SUFFERING.

TRINITY

Jesus, Spirit of God, and Father's voice from heaven. Matt. 3:16-17
In the name of the Father, Son, and Holy Spirit. Matt. 28:19
Grace of Jesus, love of God, fellowship of the Holy Spirit. 2 Cor. 13:14
(See next page for Trinity chart.)

DIVINE ATTRIBUTE	FATHER	SON	HOLY SPIRIT
Eternal	Rom. 16:26–27	Rev. 1:17	Heb. 9:14
Creator of All	Ps. 100:3	Col. 1:16	Ps. 104:30
Omnipresent	Jer. 23:24	Eph. 1:23	Ps. 139:7
All-knowing	1 John 3:20	John 21:17	1 Cor. 2:10
Acts Supernaturally	Eph. 1:5	Matt. 8:3	1 Cor. 12:11
Gives Life	Gen. 1:11–31	John 1:4	Rom. 8:10–11
Strengthens Believers	Ps. 138:3	Phil. 4:13	Eph. 3:16

TRIUMPHAL ENTRY

Jesus' entry into Jerusalem. Matt. 21:1–11; Mark 11:1–11; Luke 19:29–44; John 12:12–19

TRUMPETS

Wall fell with trumpets sound. Josh. 6:20
The last trumpet. 1 Cor. 15:52
The trumpet call of God. 1 Thess. 4:16
Seven angels with trumpets. Rev. 8:6

TRUST

Don't trust in earthly power. Ps. 20:7
Commit your way to God. Ps. 37:5
Trust with all your heart. Prov. 3:5
Put your trust in God. Isa. 8:17
"Trust in God, trust also in me." John 14:1

TRUTH

"Guide me in your truth." Ps. 25:5
Worship in spirit and truth. John 4:24
Truth will make you free. John 8:32
The way, truth, and life. John 14:6
Spirit of Truth. John 16:13
God's word is truth. John 17:17
Love rejoices with truth. 1 Cor. 13:6
See also HONESTY; LYING.

UNFAITHFUL

Trapped by evil desires. Prov. 11:6
Leads to destruction. Prov. 13:15
God frustrates their words. Prov. 22:12
See also FAITHFULNESS.

UNITY

It's pleasant for God's people. Ps. 133:1–2
All are one in Christ. Gal. 3:28
Keep the unity of the Spirit. Eph. 4:3
One Lord, faith, baptism. Eph. 4:5
Strive for unity. Eph. 4:13
Being of one spirit and mind. Phil. 2:2
See also DIVISION; HARMONY.

UNPARDONABLE SIN

See BLASPHEMY.

VANITY
See Arrogance; Boasting; Pride.

VEIL *See* Curtain.

VICTORY
God gives victory. Deut. 20:4
Victory belongs to the Lord. Ps. 3:8
God will swallow up death. Isa. 25:8
Victory in Jesus. 1 Cor. 15:55–57
Victory over the world. 1 John 5:4
See also Overcoming.

VINE/VINEYARD
Vineyard parables. Matt. 20:1–16; 21:28–32
Jesus, the true vine. John 15:1–8
Grapes of wrath. Rev. 14:19–20
See also Fruit.

VIOLENCE
Those who love violence. Ps. 11:5
Don't envy a violent person. Prov. 3:31
Wicked try to conceal it. Prov. 10:11
There shall be no more of it. Isa. 60:18
Kingdom suffers violence. Matt. 11:12
See also Abuse; Swords.

VIRGIN BIRTH
Prophesied in Old Testament. Isa. 7:14
Fulfilled in Jesus. Matt. 1:22–23; Luke 1:27

VIRTUE
Over all virtues, put on love. Col. 3:14
Add virtue to your faith. 2 Peter 1:5
See also Character; Goodness.

VISIONS
Young men will see visions.
Joel 2:28; Acts 2:17
See also Dreams; Prophecy.

VOWS *See* Oaths.

WAITING
Wait patiently for the Lord. Ps. 37:7
Wait for the Lord. Ps. 130:5
Those who wait on God will renew their strength. Isa. 40:31
God is good to those who wait. Lam. 3:25
Eagerly wait by faith. Gal. 5:5
See also Patience; Time/Timing.

WALKING
Walk in obedience to God. Deut. 28:9
Don't walk with the wicked. Ps. 1:1
Never walk in darkness. John 8:12
Keep in step with the Spirit. Gal. 5:25
Follow in Jesus' steps. 1 Peter 2:21
Walk in the light. 1 John 1:7
Walk in the truth. 3 John 1:4

A B C D E F G H I J K L M N O P Q R S T U V W X Y Z

WAR

God makes wars end. Ps. 46:9
Wars and rumors of wars. Mark 13:7
The war within. Rom. 7:23
See also SPIRITUAL WARFARE; SOLDIERS.

WATCHFULNESS

Watch and pray. Matt. 26:41
Be on your guard. Mark. 13:33
Be watchful and thankful. Col. 4:2
Be watchful, sober-minded. 1 Peter 5:8

WATER

Led beside the still waters. Ps. 23:2
Wells of salvation. Isa. 12:3
Living water. John 4:10
Water of eternal life. John 4:14
Rivers of living water. John 7:38; Rev. 22:17
See also THIRST.

WEAKNESS

Spirit helps us in weakness. Rom. 8:26
Bear with the weak. Rom. 15:1
God has chosen the weak things of this world. 1 Cor. 1:25–29
Sown in weakness, but raised in power. 1 Cor. 15:43
Strong when weak. 2 Cor. 12:9–10
See also FAILURES; STRENGTH.

WEALTH

God gives the ability to gain it. Deut. 8:18
It cannot save you. Ps. 49:6–9
Its deceitfulness. Matt. 13:22; Mark 4:19
See also MONEY; POSSESSIONS; RICH.

WEARINESS

We'll run and not get weary. Isa. 40:31
Word sustains the weary. Isa. 50:4
Jesus will give rest. Matt. 11:28
Don't grow tired of doing good. Gal 6:9

WEEPING

A time to weep. Eccl. 3:4
Jesus wept. John 11:35
Weep with those who weep. Rom. 12:15
See also GRIEF; TEARS.

WICKEDNESS

See EVIL; VIOLENCE.

WIDOWS

Be kind to them. Ex. 22:22
The widow's offering. Luke 21:1–4
Widows and remarriage. 1 Cor. 7:8–9
Honor widows. 1 Tim. 5:3
Look after them. James 1:27

WILDERNESS

Humbled and tested in it. Deut. 8:2
A voice calling in wilderness. John 1:23

WILL OF GOD

God's knows the plans for you. Jer. 29:11
"Your will be done." Matt. 6:10; Luke 11:2
"Not my will, but yours." Luke 22:42
Prove what is the will of God. Rom. 12:2
Understand what God's will is. Eph. 5:17
Reward for doing God's will. Heb. 10:36
Those who do it live forever. 1 John 2:17
See also DECISION MAKING; PLANNING.

WINE

Wine is a mocker. Prov. 20:1
Don't be drunk with it. Eph. 5:18
A little for your stomach. 1 Tim. 5:23
Not addicted to it. Titus 2:3
See also ALCOHOL; DRUNKENNESS.

WISDOM
Fools despise wisdom. Prov. 1:7
God gives wisdom. Prov. 2:6
It is more precious than gems. Prov. 8:11
Fear of Lord is its beginning. Prov. 9:10
Proved right by deeds. Matt. 11:19
World's wisdom is foolishness. 1 Cor. 3:19
Live wisely. Eph. 5:15
Ask God for wisdom. James 1:5

WITCHCRAFT *See* OCCULT.

WITNESSES
"You are my witnesses." Isa. 43:10
Tell how much God has done. Mark 5:19
Spirit will help you testify. Luke 12:11–12
Witnesses to the ends of earth. Acts 1:8
A great cloud of witnesses. Heb. 12:1
See also EVANGELISM; MISSIONS.

WIVES
Finding a wife is good. Prov. 18:22
An excellent wife. Prov. 31
Wife of unbelieving husband. 1 Cor. 7:14
Submit to husbands. Eph. 5:22; 1 Peter 3:1

WORD OF GOD
Hidden it in your heart. Ps. 119:11
A light to our path. Ps. 119:105
God's words are pure. Prov. 30:5
Live by word of God, not bread. Matt. 4:4
The Word made flesh. John 1:1–14
Faith by hearing the word. Rom. 10:17
The sword of the Spirit. Eph. 6:17
It is sharper than a sword. Heb. 4:12
It abides in you. 1 John 2:14
His name is called the Word. Rev. 19:13
See also PRESERVATION; SCRIPTURE.

WORDS *See* SPEECH; TONGUE.

WORK (VOCATION)
Work with your strength. Eccl. 9:10
Work heartily as if for God. Col. 3:23
Work with your hands. 1 Thess. 4:11
Provide for your family. 1 Tim. 5:8
Worker is worthy of wages. 1 Tim. 5:18

WORKS (DEEDS)
Commit to God all actions. Prov. 16:3
Created for good works. Eph. 2:9–10
Good work carried to completion. Phil 1:6
Do good deeds. 1 Tim. 6:18
Saved by mercy, not works. Titus 3:5
Faith without works is dead. James 2:26

WORLD
Everything in world is God's. Ps. 50:12
Go into all the world. Mark 16:15
God so loved the world. John 3:16–17
Jesus was loved by God before the foundation of the world. John 17:24
Greater is the one in you, than the one in the world. 1 John 4:4
See also EARTH.

WORLDLINESS
Jesus overcame the world. John 16:33
A kingdom not of this world. John 18:36
Don't be conformed to it. Rom. 12:2
Worldly wisdom. 2 Cor. 1:12
Deny worldly lusts. Titus 2:12
Friend of it, an enemy to God. James 4:4
Don't love it. 1 John 2:15–17

WORRY
Give all worry to God. Ps. 55:22
Do not worry. Matt. 6:25–26

Worry can't add a single hour to your life. Matt. 6:27; Luke 12:25
Tomorrow will worry itself. Matt. 6:34
Don't worry about what you'll say; Spirit will speak for you. Matt. 10:19–20
Do not let hearts be troubled. John 14:27
God will meet your needs. Phil. 4:19
Cast your cares upon the Lord. 1 Peter 5:7
See also Anxiety; Stress.

WORSHIP

Shall not worship graven images. Ex. 20:4
Great is the Lord and most worthy of praise. 1 Chron. 16:25
Worship even in suffering. Job 1:20–21
The beauty of God's holiness. Ps. 29:2
Come let us worship. Ps. 95:6
Everything that has breath, praise the Lord! Ps. 150:6
Empty worship. Isa. 29:13
Worship God, serve him only. Luke 4:8
We know whom we worship. John 4:22
Worship in spirit and in truth. John 4:24
Our spiritual act of worship. Rom. 12:1
See also Adoration; Praise.

WOUNDS

God binds our wounds. Ps. 147:3
Trust wounds from a friend. Prov. 27:6
Jesus' wounds heal us. Isa. 53:5; 1 Peter 2:24

WRATH OF GOD

It is poured out like fire. Nah. 1:2–6
It is being revealed. Rom. 1:18
It is coming. Col. 3:6
Grapes of wrath. Rev. 14:19
Seven bowls of wrath. Rev. 16:1
See also Judgment Day.

YEAST

God's kingdom is like it. Matt. 13:33
Hypocrisy, the Pharisees' yeast. Luke 12:1
A little goes a long way. 1 Cor. 5:6; Gal. 5:9

YES

Let your yes be yes, and your no be no. Matt. 5:37; James 5:12
God's promises are "yes." 2 Cor. 1:20

YOKE

Jesus' yoke is easy. Matt. 11:29–30
Don't be unevenly yoked. 2 Cor. 6:14
The yoke of slavery. Gal. 5:1; 1 Tim. 6:1

YOUTH

The sins of one's youth. Ps. 25:7
God renews your youth. Ps. 103:5
Don't think less of youths. 1 Tim. 4:12
Avoid youthful desires. 2 Tim. 2:22
Encourage young men. Titus 2:6

ZEAL

Be zealous for the fear of God. Prov. 23:17
Base zeal on what you know. Rom. 10:2
Always have zeal. Rom. 12:11

ZION

The holy hill of Zion. Ps. 2:6; Ps. 48:2
The Lamb stood on Mount Zion. Rev. 14:1